Heart of Wisdom

Heart of Wisdom

NEW EDITION

Avoid Pitfalls - Find the Straight Path
Experience Breakthrough - Through the Wisdom of God

KAREN WELLS

Heart of Wisdom / Revised Edition

Copyright © 2024 by Karen Wells. All rights reserved.

No part of this publication may be reproduced, stored in a retrieval system or transmitted in any way by any means, electronic, mechanical, photocopy, recording or otherwise without the prior permission of the author except as provided by USA copyright law.

The opinions expressed by the author are not necessarily those of URLink Print and Media.

1603 Capitol Ave., Suite 310 Cheyenne, Wyoming USA 82001
1-888-980-6523 | admin@urlinkpublishing.com

URLink Print and Media is committed to excellence in the publishing industry.

Book design copyright © 2024 by URLink Print and Media. All rights reserved.

Published in the United States of America
Library of Congress Control Number: 2021914893
ISBN 978-1-64753-887-3 (Paperback)
ISBN 978-1-64753-888-0 (Digital)
13.08.24

CONTENTS

SECTION ONE
About Wisdom

Chapter One	Wisdom is Calling	15
Chapter Two	Turning Toward a Better Life	19
Chapter Three	Insight for Those Seeking Wisdom	26
Chapter Four	God's Qualification for Wisdom	32
Chapter Five	Understanding False Wisdom	35
Chapter Six	False Wisdom in Action	41
Chapter Seven	Deliverance from False Wisdom	46

SECTION TWO
Wisdom For Life's Situations

Chapter Eight	Wisdom for Fighting Fear	59
Chapter Nine	Wisdom for Dealing with Guilt	73
Chapter Ten	Wisdom Regarding our Emotions	83
Chapter Eleven	Wisdom to Combat Intimidation	94
Chapter Twelve	Wisdom Concerning Flattery	101
Chapter Thirteen	Wisdom to Protect from Deception	110
Chapter Fourteen	The Revelation and Wisdom of the Five Smooth Stones	119
Chapter Fifteen	The Revelation and Wisdom of the Fear of the Lord	143

Proverbs 3:13-18 (New King James Version)
*"Happy is the man who finds wisdom, and
the man who gains understanding;
for her proceeds are better than the profits of silver,
and her gain than fine gold.
She is more precious than rubies, and all the things you may desire
cannot compare with her."*

DEDICATION

I dedicate this book to my faithful and loving
Savior Jesus Christ, who has and remains
so very forgiving and merciful. Who has kept
me through so many trials and battles.
Who has been faithful to guide me, correct
me and help me through this life.
There is no one like our God. There is no one like our King.
All praise to Him, the only wise God.

PREFACE

It is incredible that when we have conversations with God that are important, that we remember the exact time and place of that encounter with God. And such is the case with this book. I was driving to work many years ago, and I was so very frustrated and angry with myself. I was in a very unhappy relationship and was made to see very clearly that my unhappiness was the result of me making decisions without first seeking God. I was so upset with myself that I said out loud to God, *"God, if you ever get me out of this relationship, I promise that I will write a book on wisdom that will try to help foolish people like me from making stupid decisions like this that cost them dearly!"* I was sitting at the stop light in Houston in the Galleria area at San Felipe and North Post Oak. The light turned green and I drove on to work and never thought a thing about what I had said again.

Never in a million years did I imagine that God would get me out of that colossal mistake of a relationship, but He did. Never in ten million years did I imagine He would tap me on the shoulder decades later to make good on my vow to Him that I made at that stoplight on San Felipe, but He did. Never think God does not hear - He most certainly does!

So years later we were conducting Sunday Services at a hotel. A man who was staying at the hotel who had traveled from England, decided to join the service. He came up after the service and spoke to me and said, "God wants you to write a book on the topic of wisdom... I don't know what that is about but He is saying that He wants you to write.

The book will be about wisdom." I was thunderstruck! I thought, Are you kidding me? But there it was. God was wanting me to pay up on that vow I had made. I was astonished that He really wanted me to actually do this!

So here it is. A book on wisdom which I feel far from qualified to write, and is written to try to help people see that what the Word of God says is true. Wisdom is the principal thing. God desires so much that His people get it and in all their getting to get understanding. (Proverbs 4:7) This is because He wants us to avoid going down painful paths and down roads that lead only to disillusionment and heart ache.

May somewhere in the pages of this book God speak the needed wisdom you need to keep your life on track with His perfect will that you may prosper therein.

SECTION ONE
ABOUT WISDOM

Chapter One

Wisdom is Calling

Wisdom is calling us. Do you hear her? She desires to prosper us and to help us. She has been calling people for many generations, but most do not hear her. Some of us are on a reckless path. We must stop and hear Wisdom's call. Some of us will only get to the end of our lives and realize that we have missed the right way to live. We will think of all the things we wished we had done differently. Yet Wisdom's voice was calling, but was never heard above the ruckus of other voices out there in the world. There is a formal invitation from Wisdom in the Word of God to all of us. She is calling; she is crying out. She has indeed raised her voice loudly, and so she pleads, yearning for us to hear. Can you hear her? She wants to be part of our choices, our decisions, and our plans. She desires to be chosen, so we must choose her. Listen to her words addressed to all of mankind throughout the ages. Notice at the onset that she is shouting. She is shouting to be heard out of the maze of other voices out there in this thing called life. So, let's, at this moment, hear what she has to say.

Proverbs 1:20-22 (New American Standard Bible)
"Wisdom shouts in the street, she lifts her voice in the square;
at the head of the noisy streets, she cries out;
at the entrance of the gates in the city she utters her sayings:
How long, O naive ones, will you love being simple-minded?
And scoffers delight themselves in scoffing and fools hate knowledge?"

Proverbs 8:1-7 (NASB)

*"Does not wisdom call, and understanding lift up her voice?
On the top of the heights beside the way, where the paths meet,
she takes her stand; beside the gates, at the opening to
the city, at the entrance of the doors, she cries out:
'To you O men, I call, and my voice is to the sons of men.
O naive ones, understand prudence; and O fools, discern wisdom.
Listen, for I shall speak noble things; and the opening
of my lips will produce right things.
For my mouth will utter truth;"*

Yet Folly Calls Also

From another pinnacle calls another voice in life. She is the opposite of Wisdom, and her name is Folly. Folly will ruin your life. She thinks she has the way and that everyone else does not. She elevates herself by pride and foolishness not knowing she is the laughing stock of heaven. All who take her path are in for a rude awakening. In the end, she will embarrass and shame us. Folly is as blind as a bat and doesn't know it. Many listen to Folly because she seems to have all the answers. She sure acts like she does, but Folly is a false voice sent to trip us up. It's time to recognize her and call her what she is: a big fake, an imposter, a blaring blow horn. Oh, don't misunderstand me, she talks it up good, and she's emphatic, but don't be fooled, she is a mess and so is her pathway. Her way is scattered with broken things and unfulfilled dreams of those who have followed her, thinking they are on the inside track and that they have it made. In the end, only futility, devastation, and loss are the reward. We must be aware of Folly. It's time to wake up and get a hold of our lives where Folly is concerned. Here is the discourse of Folly in the word of God, and we can see also that her voice calls loudly to us as well.

Proverbs 9:13-18 (NASB)
"The woman folly is boisterous; she is naive and knows nothing.
She sits at the doorway of her house, on a
seat by the high places of the city,
calling to those who pass by, who are making their paths straight:
'Whoever is naive, let him turn in here, and to
him who lacks understanding she says,
'Stolen water is sweet; and bread eaten in secret is pleasant.'
But he does not know that the dead are there, that
her guests are in the depths of Sheol."

A few poor decisions, several difficult circumstances, and throw in some dire consequences and it should dawn on us that we have been listening to none other than the voice of Folly. The day soon comes when we wake up, as the prodigal son did, in the pig pen of our life and say, "What am I doing here and how did I get to this place?" I'll tell you how you got to that place; you arrived at that place because of Folly. She is your problem, your headache, your burning issue, and has been for quite some time now. And this is the thing: your life cannot be a mess for no reason. You need to take stock as the prodigal son did and begin to ask for the right way. The prodigal son had a father and so do we. If our earthly father was not a man of wisdom, we surely have a Heavenly Father who will be delighted to pick us up, dust us off, and set us on the right path. It's called Wisdom's path. Wisdom's voice may have seemed soft and boring to us when we were younger, but it was the right voice. If we had sought Wisdom out and listened when she presented herself to us, we might have had a better outcome. Let's face it, any outcome is better than Folly's outcome. And so now we come to the place of the principal thing in life. The Word of God says that the principal and most important thing is wisdom. God's wisdom shall not fail us. God's wisdom profits all who acquire it. Are you ready for wisdom's counsel? Are you tired of a failed life that lacks wisdom's input? Then come along and let us take a walk down wisdom's path together.

Proverbs 4: 7-9 (New King James Version)
"Wisdom is the principal thing; therefore, get wisdom.
And in all your getting, get understanding.
Exalt her, and she will promote you; she will
bring you honor, when you embrace her.
She will place on your head an ornament of grace;
a crown of glory she will deliver to you."

Chapter Two

Turning Toward a Better Life

Proverbs 3: 5-6 (NASB)
"Trust in the Lord with all your heart and do not lean on your own understanding. In all your ways acknowledge Him, and He will make your paths straight."

It Starts by Acknowledging Him

The key word that stands out to me in this scripture is the word acknowledge. Why? Because it is what God is looking for from us. He wants us to acknowledge Him. So often we live our lives with God on the sidelines until we need Him in some desperate way to, all of a sudden, do something. We can in essence use God as a "fix it" man. He can fix what is broken, mend what is torn, undo what was done, or do whatever else is needed, all due to our lack of seeking Him and allowing Him to be Lord. This kind of thinking and habitual behavior will get us into trouble. Strolling along through life and expecting God to sweep up behind us with a broom to clean up all our avoidable messes is not exactly what God had in mind for His people, and yet this is the way many of us live much of the time. The fact is there comes a time when God will call us into more maturity and accountability. Pretty soon, He will start leaving the messes for all to see and for us to clean up. This is the wonderful land of bad consequences due to irresponsible living. Bad consequences can give us the reality check we may need to cause us to, as the Bible says, "Consider our ways." (Haggai 1:7) Haggai, the prophet, was sent by God to let Israel know that their negative consequences were due to them neglecting the priorities of God. Consequently, God called for a drought on their land and that drought hit the mountains, the grain, the new wine, the oil, and whatever else the ground brought forth. The drought also negatively, in turn, affected the livestock and all the labor of their hands. Ouch! Wisely, the people regrouped and redirected themselves by "acknowledging" God, and so they experienced an awesome turnaround.

Our Own Ways Versus God's Ways

Unfortunately, many times we do not always reflect, re-direct, and change our ways. We instead, can be in denial or choose to avoid the issue. This only prolongs the pain of the inevitable consequence. God forgives us as we repent but He does not always remove the consequence. Other times when we have an issue we can resort to blaming something or someone rather than looking inward into our own soul. This is known as the "beam in the eye syndrome" that Jesus mentioned saying: "Why do you see the speck that is in your brother's eye, but do not see the beam that is in your own eye?" (Luke 6:41) That is a sure sign it is time to look in the mirror. Another trap we can fall into, when we fail to connect with God is the pit of self-pity. It is not hard to land there and draw others to us so that they may feel sorry for us in our horrible plight whatever it may be. It is then that some well meaning person can serve as an enabler rather than what is truly needed: a bonafide truth-giver who is brave enough to unveil what needs to be dealt with. One such truth-giver was the prophet Nathan. King David, steeped miles high in his own sins, could not see himself due to the deep darkness that sin brings, but Nathan brilliantly cast the light causing King David to see himself, paving the way towards King David's much needed repentance and restoration.

Are We Ready to Really Listen?

God is always ready to set us back on the right path. Sometimes He causes us to catch ourselves so that we can acknowledge Him and find the straight path, or sometimes He will send people that are His messengers of truth, or sometimes He will send circumstances to finally get our attention that things are out of order with Him. Whatever the case, the Holy Spirit is at work quietly wooing us and waiting for us. He waits until we are positioned to listen. He wisely waits until our soul is played out, defeated, finished, and dead, in the sense of the foolish, self-centered course it was on. Then, with our spiritual ears finally open and our heart inclined to (here's the word) 'acknowledge Him,' we can begin to receive some sound wisdom in the form of counsel. It is only His mercy that causes God to wait so patiently for us, not only until we are ready to hear what needs to be heard, but also ready to obey what is heard the same.

Isaiah 30:18 (NKJV)
"Therefore, the Lord will wait, that He may be gracious to you;
And therefore He will be exalted, that He may have mercy on you."

If He spoke sooner, we may hear it and not obey it, and He would not want us to dig yet a deeper pit for ourselves through disobedience to His counsel. So, He waits until we are ready. Only when we acknowledge God can we receive the blessings of a straight path that He has for us and get off the crooked one.

The Blessing of the Straight Path

Proverbs 3:6 (NASB)
"…. in all your ways acknowledge Him, and
He will make your paths straight."

One cannot appreciate the blessing of the straight path until one has lived life on the crooked one.

I, for one, have experienced both and can wholeheartedly assure you that the straight path is the only way to go. Straight, translated from the Hebrew (3474), *Yasher* translated means to be level, straight, right, tranquil, to be made even, and beat out flat. The scripture states that God will make our paths straight. The revelation here is that God Himself, as we choose to acknowledge Him in all our ways, will:

1.) Level our path
2.) Make our path convenient
3.) Make our path peaceful
4.) Even go to the trouble of beating down the bumps along the way!

The straight path is a path on which God has removed the obstacles. It is the path where God has gone before us.

> *Proverbs 4:11-12 (Berean Study Bible)*
> *"I will guide you in the way of wisdom;*
> *I will lead you on straight paths. When you walk, your steps will not be impeded; when you run, you will not stumble."*

The Rickety Bridge of Our Own Understanding

We must consider God before we cross bridges and make turns in the road of life, because life has a funny way of coming up short so much of the time. The fact of the matter is, God is busy at work in our lives breaking down the structures of our reliance on ourselves so that we can come to the place of completely relying, trusting, and leaning on Him. In fact, He is already busy at work to intentionally dismantle our finest plans in this regard. Why would God do a thing like this? Well, God is not a tag-along God. God's job is to lead and not to follow. Many of us can assume God is leading or blessing us as we take the helm of our lives, but that so much of the time is not the case.

Like Sheep We Have Our Nose to the Ground Most of the Time

God clearly is a god of guidance. In scripture He describes us metaphorically as sheep. Forget the endearing thoughts you have about how tender it is of God to think of us as sheep and those fond memories you have of those cute, little, fluffy sheep you see on the Dayspring cards. A thorough study of sheep brought me to the sober reality that sheep are not among the smartest of animals. Sheep graze along fields with their noses to the ground allowing their appetites to lead them wherever they go. They become completely absorbed, sniffing the ground, and wander off wherever their noses will take them. Pretty soon, they look up, look around, and say, "Hmmm, how did I get here? Where did everybody go? Where's the shepherd? Isn't He supposed to be watching over me?" Is this not how we are? We lift our heads up when we have finished our fleshly fill and ask, "How in the world did I arrive here? Where is everybody? Where is the presence of God?" Need I say more? The fact is, sheep are essentially helpless and directionless without a shepherd to keep them out of trouble. Even with a shepherd, sheep get themselves into a lot of predicaments! Yet, we often have to learn this truth the hard way. Let us look up and acknowledge the Lord in our lives. Let us just plain look up and let us look to God, the Author and Finisher of our faith. From whatever place we have been and no matter how bumpy the ride, one of God's greatest longings is that we come to know and trust in Him fully and completely.

Trusting in the Lord

Trust. It is one of those words that sounds so noble and wonderful when it is read and thought about from afar, but when our number is up and we are really called upon to actually trust, it can be a place where our mettle is truly tested. I believe we are all on the path of learning to trust God and that as we walk further and further with the Lord, we can expect our trust in God will be tested again and again. Webster's definition of trust is, "The assured reliance on the character, ability, strength or truth of someone or something." Wow! The "assured reliance" is the part that we all want to get to with God. What is this trust thing really all about? The issue of trust with God I've come to learn, only becomes more secure in proportion to our intimacy with Him. This is because trust essentially is a relationship word. If you trust someone, chances are you are in close relationship with them. You have spent enough time with them to know they can be - trusted.

Don't be Afraid - Just Look Down

At one point in my life, it seemed the bottom was falling out. Relationships had fallen away that I had at one time been able to count on, or so I thought. I was in a new city and literally everything was unfamiliar. I remember it seemed that those that had moved on in the world were laughing at me. I was now feeling very alone and scared in my Christian walk, which was very new to me at the time. And then the Lord in His compassions, which fail not, gave me a vision. I was on a very high mountain cliff. There was no turning back and moving forward had no apparent path. Then I heard the words, "Don't be afraid, just look down." I was terrified to look down because it was so high and precarious, but I made myself look down and there I saw a huge hand that my bare feet were resting on. The people of the world, of which I was no longer a part, were on the "safe" ground across the way with a picket fence on their side. They seemed to be so well protected while I was in this impossible place that seemed to have no safe way through. But there I saw God's hand underneath me being the literal path for me at that very difficult and lonely time in my life. God was my path, no longer the world. What a God of comfort and guidance we have. That vision held me in His trust for many months as I made the huge and difficult transitions that were needed at that time. I learned that when our "trust tank" gets on empty, there is a God who steps in to a place of intimacy with us that no one else could possible know. Trust is not blind. It is intrinsically founded on experience after experience with God proving Himself to be faithful and true.

Really Trusting is a Matter of the Heart

The first part of Proverbs 3:5, says, *"Trust the Lord with all your heart and lean not on your own understanding..."* Notice that we trust with the heart and not our mind. I think this is why it is so painful to trust and be disappointed or betrayed because we trust with the heart. God is very interested in having a heart relationship with us. As we come to know God, we learn more and more that He can be trusted. I discovered something recently in the Word of God that I would like to share because it has to do with how much God desires to develop a close abiding relationship with us. It was found in Proverbs 3:32, which says, *"For the devious are an abomination to the Lord, but He is intimate with the upright."* I was drawn to the word 'intimate', which in Hebrew is the word *'cowd'* which means a couch, a cushion, a pillow, a friendly conversation among friends. I guess this is where we get the idiom, "pillow talk." So we can say, as far as our relationship with God is concerned, that He desires a "pillow talk" relationship with us. I venture to say that it is in these "pillow talk" times with God that we come into true intimacy with Him. It is then that we can enter into the awesome place of truly trusting Him with all of our heart. As we learn to trust the Lord, we will lean more and more on the arm of our Savior concerning our choices and decisions. It was Moses who said by his meekness of spirit in Exodus 33:15, "... If Your presence does not go with us, do not lead us up from here ..." Moses truly knew all about the presence of God. And one cannot know the presence of God unless they become intimate with Him. Moses did not want to venture out into the future without the Lord. He insisted on only going forth with His presence. The one who truly follows God dares not proceed the One called to go before.

Chapter Three

Insight for Those Seeking Wisdom

Proverbs 4:7 (New International Version)
"The beginning of wisdom is this: Get wisdom.
Though it cost all you have, get understanding."

Proverbs 4:7 (Amplified)
"The beginning of Wisdom is: Get Wisdom (skillful and godly wisdom)!
[For skillful and godly Wisdom is the principal thing.]
And with all you have gotten, get understanding
(discernment, comprehension, and interpretation)."

Getting Rid of Mistaken Notions

Wisdom is something we choose to walk in. It does not just fall on us. We can be under the mistaken notion that because we are born again, spirit-filled Christians, God will automatically guide us and prevent us from making mistakes. This cannot be farther from the truth. From the book of Genesis until now, God has sat back and let man be responsible for his own choices. In fact, right from the beginning we can see in the book of Genesis that God did not endow an automatic dispensing of wisdom to mankind so that forevermore man would be mercifully prevented from making mistakes and be released from having to bear the pain of harmful consequences. Eve chose to forsake God's wisdom, which came in the form of instruction, and instead of intervening to prevent disaster, God restrained Himself. He sat back and let the whole thing happen. I make these statements due to the fact that there are many mistaken notions and fallacies out there among believers that God has some kind of automatic "protection plan" in place whether we are choosing the way of wisdom or not. Let us make no mistake here and soberly realize that God has given us everything we need to live wisely, but He has also given us the choice and the great encouragement and admonishment to avidly pursue His wisdom as a determined course in this life. In fact, God goes further than that; He has given us the book of Proverbs, which is basically a book on how to stay out of trouble and how to avoid sordid pitfalls in life. In it, God entreats us strongly to get wisdom and to get understanding. Furthermore, the book of Proverbs literally begs us to obtain these virtues but we are still left, very much, on our own to make the actual choice. No, wisdom is not automatically part of the Christian's "care-package." It is the Christian's responsibility to, as the Bible says, "get it." (Prov. 4:7) Great blessing is gained by those who succeed in apprehending it. At the same time, the Word of God tells us that it is to our great detriment to neglect to find wisdom. In a single scripture, we can see the benefit of obtaining wisdom and also at the same time see the great disadvantage of failing to find it.

Proverbs 8:34-36 (NIV)
"Blessed are those who listen to me, watching daily at my doors, waiting at my doorway. For those who find me find life and receive favor from the Lord. But those who fail to find me harm themselves;"

In this scripture, we see that failing to find wisdom will harm us; that we will, in fact, suffer unnecessary losses and endure unnecessary and avoidable pain. So, let's journey together and understand what God's wisdom is all about and respond to God's earnest plea to get the heavenly wisdom we need and that has been made available to each of us.

Moving in Agreement with the Activities of Heaven and God

James 3:13 (NASB)
"Who among you is wise and understanding?
Let him show by his good behavior his
deeds in the gentleness of wisdom."

The word "wise" in this text comes from the Greek word *Sophia* (4678), which means, "One who knows how to regulate his course in view of, (in keeping with), the movements of heaven and God."

So what this is saying is that the one who is living by heavenly wisdom is moving with or alongside the activities of heaven. Another way of saying this would be that one is flowing in keeping with heaven's agenda - when heaven and earth can meet in agreement to accomplish things for God. So, this scripture is asking, *"Who is the one who is flowing alongside heaven in keeping with the movements of God?"* The above scripture also says you can tell those who are. They can be observed. They are the ones who demonstrate good behavior with their deeds being performed in the gentleness of wisdom. (Other translations say, in the humility of wisdom). The Amplified Version says, *"...with the [unobtrusive] humility [which is the proper attribute] of true wisdom."*

What is the Gentleness of Wisdom?

What does all this mean? What this is saying is that even though you have the power of the truth and insight that God has given you from heaven, true wisdom is proven by how it is lived out. It is not just the insight that makes us wise, it is the manner in which we express it. For instance, the gentleness of wisdom is the ability to not only speak the truth, but to speak the truth at the right time, in the right measure, for the right reason, and in the right way. Let's think of some examples. Joseph, in the book of Genesis, received some powerful truths from God in the form of dreams which foretold his future of prominence and his subsequent position over his brothers. Although he had powerful prophetic insight (a magnificent vision for his future), the gentleness of wisdom was not part of his character yet. Instead, he was somewhat boastful, presumptuous, and obnoxious from his family's point of view. No matter how excited a person may be about what God has truly shown them, it would serve us all well to share sacred revelations and impartations such as these with only a select few. Joseph missed all the cues due to being wrapped up in the excitement of what he had received from God. The actual truth was that his ornery brothers were fed up with the rantings of his latest spiritual experience of yet another dream. They soon began to mock him ruthlessly. The fact is, even in the church, there are not many who are that genuinely excited about the elevation and promotion of another person. And in Joseph's case it was no different. The revealing of the disclosures from heaven to his brothers only worked to fuel the raging fires of jealousy, envy, and strife. Unwisely stoking those fires brought severe persecution, hardship, and bondage into Joseph's life. He ended up paying dearly for his lack of prudence and his lack of gentleness of wisdom. It was only after many years of suffering and hard times that Joseph came into full maturity, gaining, with his anointed gifts and insights, the "gentleness" of wisdom; it was only then that God could entrust him with the great authority and responsibility of the call that was on his life. Although Joseph had been correct in his revelatory insight, (it was the truth after all), it was spoiled through sharing it with those who would never receive it, and would only seek with all their might to abuse and spoil any hope of the sacred vision from coming to pass. Truth is not always wise to share. It takes a certain strength of humility to hide God's treasures within one's own heart. Though revelation may be bursting inside of us to come out, can we, with meekness and humility, hold into ourselves the secret sacred things of God, and thereby prosper and flow with God in the timing of His higher ways?

Revelation Comes to Mary

Regarding Mary the mother of Jesus, there is no other person in the Bible called upon to contain such magnificent revelation. Upon her tremendous spiritual encounters and disclosures from God, that she was to conceive the Son of God, she was very wise to move in the gentleness of wisdom by simply pondering these incredible things in her heart. Remember, the gentleness of wisdom is the ability not only to speak the revelatory truth, but to speak this kind of truth at the right time, in the right measure, for the right reason and in the right way. When we achieve this we are moving in keeping with heaven and God's highest purposes in any given situation. Mary was not interested in putting herself out there. She was not heady, boastful, intrusive, all knowing, but quite the opposite. We see Mary displaying the attributes of *Sophia* wisdom; she is both wise and understanding.

Luke 2:19 (BSB)
"But Mary treasured up all these things and pondered them in her heart."

When we are filled to the brim with some amazing things God has shown us, do we have the gentleness of wisdom to contain and carry it out in the character of Christ? The crowning hallmark of heavenly wisdom is indeed humility. When our soul-man is truly yielded and submitted to the Holy Spirit, we will walk in this type of grace and maturity. In the book of Genesis, it took Joseph many years, but God finally did establish him with great authority and into the high position in Egypt that He called him to, but not without a certain humility fixed firmly in place in his heart after years of living in the crucible of a prison place and thinking of himself as forgotten with no hope for any redeemable future. But God was at work. The story teaches us that no matter what others may do to try and ruin your call, God in the end will have His way. His servant will be sorely tried but come forth unscathed. All praise to God.

Defining Godly Wisdom

Godly wisdom is the divine insight into the true nature of a thing and the ability to discern the course of action to take regarding that issue.

Godly wisdom has two parts. The first part of wisdom is the divine insight that God initially gives us.

Proverbs 2:6 (NKJV)
"For the Lord gives wisdom; from His mouth come knowledge and understanding."

The second part of wisdom is understanding the course of action to take regarding the insight that has been given. Many of us get so excited when God imparts heavenly insight, that we go off half-cocked into that situation with the revelational insight, but then fail in the application because we release it our way and not God's way, in our time and not God's time. In these ways, we have failed to seek God for the fulness of wisdom needed. Therefore, the impartation of heavenly wisdom and insight from God depend desperately on a wise vessel from which that wisdom may flow or else, all is lost and contaminated by our own foolish tampering in its personal motive, delivery, and or application. Hence, we can say as Daniel has said:

Daniel 2:21 (NKJV)
"... He gives wisdom to the wise and knowledge to those who have understanding."

Chapter Four

God's Qualification for Wisdom

Proverbs 11:2 (BSB)
"When pride comes, disgrace follows, but with humility comes wisdom."

What does humility have to do with wisdom? Apparently, a great deal. Thus, it deserves attention in our quest for attaining the wisdom or mind of God. The essential fact is, with God one cannot gain wisdom without humility. The scripture says, "...with humility comes wisdom." It would stand to reason then that if we are wanting wisdom to come, we would need to humble ourself before God in order to receive it. We, of course, can gain earthly wisdom any number of ways. But in order to receive godly wisdom, the posture of humility is needed. This is also echoed from the book of James as well, where the person in a great trial would be encouraged to ask God for wisdom and to ask in faith, and then it is promised that God would supply the needed wisdom for the dire situation at hand (James 1:5-6). Asking automatically places us in a humble mindset, and it is in this place that one can expect God to respond. If we miss the humility requirement, we will in turn gain no viable response from heaven. I'm not sure if we can afford that, given the many challenges that come before us in this life. The fact is, humility is the key that opens the door for God to supply the needed wisdom we need for any of our life situations at any given time. Additionally, Psalm 25 shares with us that there is only one kind of person that qualifies, in God's mind, to receive His wisdom of divine guidance and instruction. It is not just anyone that approaches Him who meets the grade. According to the scripture, the person that qualifies for God's guidance and instruction is, unequivocally, the humble person.

> *Psalm 25:9 (NKJV)*
> *"The humble He guides in justice, and the humble He teaches His way."*

We are Called to Put on Humility and to Wear it

Humility is something the Christian is called to put on and to be clothed in. Humility serves as a type of covering for the Christian. It is not a militant protection as in the armor of God mentioned in Ephesians 6, but it is a robe of distinction recognized by God and the entire spirit realm as well. It is like wearing a sign that says, "I walk in the character of Christ." It's a mark and a sign that Christ-like-ness has just walked into the room or situation.

> *Colossians 3:12 (NKJV)*
> *"Therefore, as the elect of God, holy and beloved,*
> *put on tender mercies, kindness,*
> *humility, meekness, long-suffering;"*

> *1 Peter 5:5 (NKJV)*
> *"Likewise, you younger people, submit yourselves to your elders.*
> *Yes, all of you be submissive to one another, and be clothed with humility,*
> *for 'God resists the proud, but gives grace to the humble.'"*

Humility is not comfortable to the flesh, and it is not something a person is attracted to put on. But it comes to grow in value to the believer as he or she matures. He or she finds that a certain grace or favor accompany them when they have it on versus when they do not. Pride, on the other hand, is a flashy outfit that is sure to be noticed and in that, we will have our reward. But humility is a lowly coat. It draws no attention at all. Our flesh will not gain the attention it craves, but somehow from within ourselves, with the lowly coat of humility on, we know that we are right where we need to be, because now the light of Christ can be seen and we, ourselves, not. John the Baptist says it so well by saying, "He must be greater and I must be less." (John 3:30)

The Peril of the Proud

There is a passage of scripture that depicts the peril of the proud. This passage also reveals the Lord's great sadness and agony for one who has fallen into pride's rugged path of loss and ruin. It serves as a vivid warning and a sobering wake up call to those of us that would inadvertently cast off our lowly cloak of humility for the boastful coat pride. Pride's insidious nature blinds us and uncovers us and finishes the job by leading us into certain captivity that is filled with darkness. Let us read these words and hear the Lord's lament as He stands by and watches His own stumble.

Jeremiah 13:15-17 (NKJV)
"Hear and give ear: Do not be proud, for the Lord has spoken.
Give glory to the Lord your God before He causes
darkness, and before your feet stumble on the dark
mountains, and while you are looking for light,
He turns it into the shadow of death and makes it dense darkness.
But if you will not hear it, My soul will weep in secret for your pride;
My eyes will weep bitterly and run down with tears,
because the Lord's flock has been taken captive."

Chapter Five
Understanding False Wisdom

Beware of False Wisdom

The Bible says there are two kinds of wisdom, godly wisdom and false or earthly wisdom. At any given time, we are either flowing in one or the other. As believers, we need to become aware of the two and recognize which kind of wisdom we are moving in. This is paramount because one is a counterfeit. It may feel right at the time, but it is not derived of the Spirit. This counterfeit wisdom will prove false and fruitless, and even ruin our life if we choose to follow its path, especially because it can be progressive in nature. Let us look into this powerful scripture for further insight into false wisdom.

James 3:14-16 (NKJV)
"But if you have bitter envy and self-seeking in your hearts, do not boast and lie against the truth. This wisdom does not descend from above but is earthly, sensual, demonic. For where envy and self-seeking exist, confusion and every evil thing are there."

The Three Progressive Levels of False Wisdom are:

1.) Earthly wisdom
2.) Sensual wisdom
3.) Demonic wisdom

1. EARTHLY WISDOM

Earthly wisdom, mentioned in the book of James, bases itself on limited human knowledge and does not seek God for anything higher. It is running on its own steam so to speak, and only by the very limited earthly-based knowledge of fallen man. Earthly wisdom does not desire God's input on anything. It is self-sufficient and self-led. It is confident in its own ability without God's input. This level of false wisdom is not evil, but it is not redemptive either. In other words, it is not entirely without merit, and one can gain from it, but in a difficult situation earthly wisdom most likely will fail you. The scripture states, "My people are destroyed for lack of knowledge." (Hosea 4:6). Further study of the Hebrew translation unpacks this scripture in this way, "My people are destroyed for lack of redemptive revelations of God." Redemptive means saving. In other words, the revelation or revealing of God would have served to save the people and benefit them, but alas, since heavenly wisdom was not sought to gain the knowledge of God, the people were destroyed for lack of it. They just did not have nor did they seek God for the needed revelation that He had for them. God always has insight for His own. Without the knowledge, or saving revelation(s) of God, people are eventually led into captivity and bondage and from that point, they are destroyed. The word "destroyed" here means in actuality, "go into captivity and bondage." We can see this time and again as we track Israel's history. Israel, in their sin of forgetting God and going their own way, was always first led into captivity under a cruel ruler, and then their final end was destruction except for a small remnant by the mercies of God. So, with this in mind, this scripture in the book of Hosea can now read like this: "My people are destroyed, (go into bondage and captivity perishing to their destruction), for lack of redemptive (saving) revelations of God." Notice further how this scripture is not speaking about just any people - but God's people - His very own. God watches them enter into bondage and captivity because they have failed to receive or apprehend needed revelation or wisdom from Him. This places His people out from under His care because they have chosen to go their own way, or they have carelessly and unwisely rejected His wisdom, thinking their own plans and ways were better.

Earthly Wisdom is Worldly

In further describing earthly wisdom, it pertains only to this world and is limited solely to the ways of this world. It is worldly thinking and worldly problem solving. This is where man was before he was born again, with his base nature leading the way. This is where we also remain if we choose not to attain to the higher ways of God in our lives. The apostle Paul admonishes the Corinthians for not attaining past their immature worldly state, which typifies the mindset of those who move in the carnality of earthly wisdom to the core.

1 Corinthians 3:1-3 (NKJV)
"And I brethren, could not speak to you as to spiritual
people but as to carnal, as to babes in Christ.
I fed you with milk and not with solid food; for
until now you were not able to receive it,
and even now you are still not able; for you are still carnal.
For where there are envy, strife, and divisions
among you, are you not carnal
and behaving like mere men?"

2. SENSUAL "SOULISH" WISDOM

Soulish wisdom, in its way of thinking and doing, begins to attract and summon demons into one's life. It does so because the behaviors of the flesh are becoming wholly embraced. When darkness sees that a person is personally invested in certain vices of their flesh, it knows then that there is great opportunity to use that person for the purposes of the kingdom of darkness, even if that person calls themselves a Christian. For example, Saul was of this type. He continually yielded himself to his fleshly ways and refused to change his thinking and behavior to be in alignment with what God desired. This eventually resulted in him becoming sorely tormented and demonized.

Soulish Wisdom Attracts the Demonic

Essentially, the person flowing in soulish wisdom does not have his or her soul rightly relating to God under the direction of the Holy Spirit. The independent actions of the soul deprive him or her of true intimacy with God. These same independent actions of his or her soul also place him or her outside of the sanctions of God. This is what makes a person vulnerable to being satanically empowered or inclined, with or without their knowledge. This person many times may know scripture, but in essence he or she is clearly not governed by scripture. Clearly this is dangerous territory. Fleshly inclinations left unchecked with no resolve to turn and repent, provide an open door to evil spirits who are all the while salivating and panting to hook themselves into the flaming fleshly tendencies of the person. The powers of darkness are attracted to those who maneuver by the flesh and work through their desires and problems by means of competition, strife, resentment, bitterness, manipulation, jealousy, anger and a host of other fleshly vices versus solving and responding to life issues by way of what scripture dictates and by what the Holy Spirit desires. There is a difference though, between those who are immature in their faith having not crucified their flesh yet in certain areas of their lives versus those who use fleshly vices on purpose to deceive, achieve and manipulate to get their way for personal gain. In either case though, when we choose fleshly vices as a means to promote self, or in abuse for power, or to intentional harm or a host of other wrong agendas, we have now stepped outside of God's grace and protection zone. This kind of persistent living is what will bring us into the third stage of false wisdom which involves full blown demonization.

3. DEMONIC WISDOM

At this level, demons have been attracted to the habitual sin-based attitudes and lifestyle of a person. Simply said, sin attracts demons. It is their feeding ground. Ongoing, habitual, willful, defiant sin provides the welcome sign on the door of our lives that evil spirits need to gain legal access to work through us and in us. Where these vices of the flesh once served oneself very well and were pleasurable, at this level the demonic power will now seek to use the person in further ways to promote satanic agendas that one may or may not be aware of. Whether a person is aware or not, they have now come under the bondage and control of the powers of darkness. This scripture in the book of Second Timothy expresses this state very well:

2 Timothy 2:26 (NKJV)
"…that they may come to their senses and escape the snare of the devil, having been taken captive by him to do his will."

Suffice it to say, there is a crossing over that happens much like what happened to Samson. He kept playing in the sandbox of the flesh, carrying the anointing into the practice of sin thinking, I suppose, because he was so set apart and anointed, that he would be protected. He thought he could handle Delilah but she handled him. He is one of the saddest cases of a soul gone wrong in the Bible besides Saul. Let us understand that both were men who knew God and served God. This should be a sobering wake up call to the church.

Unless a person perceives the dark spirits or someone has the boldness to confront them in love, and they thereby repent for allowing the access through their sin(s), they will not be free. I need to add this as well: repenting is not just confessing our sin, repenting means turning away from it as well. The church understands the confessional part, but I am not sure we understand the turning away part as well.

The Realm of Demonic Bondage

If the person does not repent, they will find themselves experiencing increasing pressure to perform in keeping with those demonic inclinations, thoughts, and voices going on in their heads. Those spirits will hammer and hammer to be obeyed and followed. Some people will obey just to get relief. But the backside of that is they will have to deal with the misery of what they did that was demonically provoked. In the case that they did not obey the demonic provocation, they will be harrassed by those demons with increased torment and or affliction or some other payback retaliation from the realm of darkness.

God is faithful. If we sincerely cry out to Him in our distressing and miserable place, He will hear and help us to be set free. That's what Jesus came to do, to set the captives free. May God be praised now and forevermore.

Note: A Christian cannot be possessed by demons, but a Christian who practices habitual sin willfully, who remains unrepentant, who continues in known and willful disobedience and rebellion can easily encounter the influence, oppression, torment, bondage, harassment, and captivity of demon powers. The only reason these demon powers have access to cling or to attach to an individual is because these evil spirits have located open doors of habitual sin that have in turn created entrances into the person's life.

Chapter Six

False Wisdom in Action

Because this subject on false wisdom is so important, I feel led to have us see, in the Word of God, those who have fallen in this way. There are two men in the Bible that highlight for us the course of false wisdom. Both of these men had a relationship with God. Both of these men heard the voice and instruction of God. Both of these men were given opportunity by God to change and were warned by God to alter the direction they were going in. But both refused. Both came to a crossroads and made the fateful choice to choose the way of self over the way of God. Both took the false wisdom way.

The Man Who Wouldn't Change

The story of Cain and Abel gives us the contrast of two men: one who was rightly relating to God and one man who was not rightly relating to God. The story takes place in Genesis 4 where both men provided God with an offering. One was received by God and one clearly was not. Many dissertations exist as to exactly why God did not receive Cain's offering and why He did receive Abel's. I won't belabor that issue here. But, I do want us to zero in on Cain's response to God's refusal to accept his offering.

Genesis 4:4-7 (NKJV)
*"... And the Lord respected Abel and his offering, but
He did not respect Cain and his offering.
And Cain was very angry, and his countenance
fell. So, the Lord said to Cain,
'Why are you angry? And why has your countenance fallen?
If you do well, will you not be accepted? And if
you do not do well, sin lies at the door.
And its desire is for you, but you should rule over it."*

So, we see here: God is gracious, wanting Cain to receive the same benefit as his brother Abel. So much so that He tells him what is needed to achieve the same result. But, unfortunately, Cain chose a path independent of God's wisdom and went ahead in his own false wisdom and thinking. There is no other place I can recall in scripture where we see, behind the scenes so to speak, someone at the very crossroads of this kind of decision. There is no question that Cain knew what the right thing to do was in order to gain the favor and blessing of God. God was in every way saying to Cain, "I strongly suggest that you not take the way of your lower flesh nature in a kind of thinking that will not prosper you." It is a moment of divine opportunity to change, to rethink what one is about to do. God is right there, it's a Kodak moment, heaven is peering from it's balconies, but Cain will have none of it. God lets him know that sin lies at the door. What a moment this is! Cain is teetering between the blessing of God or the curse.

Deuteronomy 30:19 (New Living Translation)
*"Today I have given you the choice between life
and death, between blessings and curses.
Now I call on heaven and earth to witness the choice you make.
Oh, that you would choose life, so that you
and your descendants might live!"*

We all yearn for Cain to simply choose the blessing, but it seems he will not. And God will not go against our will. It is interesting the words God uses to warn Cain saying: "...*sin lies at the door and its desire is for you.*" In another translation it says, "...sin is crouching at the door..." (Gen.4:7). The Hebrew word here for 'crouching' is an ancient Babylonian word which referred to an evil spirit crouching at the door waiting to be given the opportunity to leap inside the house. The house, of course, would be us, since we are called in scripture a temple of the Lord. So God was in essence saying, *"Hey Cain, by the way, there is a demon right next to you, right now that will enter you if you do not change your course!"* But Cain did not want to give up his anger and resentment. He would not change his resolve. When we do this, we also will provide a sure opening for the enemy to come in to our temple as well and ruin our lives, all for the sake of choosing what is Biblically called false wisdom.

Ephesians 4:26-27 (NKJV)
"Be angry, and do not sin: do not let the sun go down on your wrath, nor give place to the devil."

The Man with the Jealous Eye

It was a beautiful relationship and then things took a wicked turn. I am sure you have encountered this in relationships with people. This happened in the relationship between David and Saul.

One day, a little jig of a tune could be heard coming towards King Saul as he walked down the pathway to greet his people. *It sounds like victory has come my way,* he thought, *what a wonderful thing! Look, everyone is so happy that they are dancing as well!* Soon the words came to be clearer as he drew closer and closer. "Saul has slain his thousands..." his face lit up with glee hearing his name sung and lifted high into the air for all to hear and marvel about. But then, after gloating over the words he had heard about himself, it became apparent what the rest of the lyrics were, " .... and David his ten thousands." *Wait a minute,* he thought, *this is not right! Since when is David given place with my name and noted more than I? I am the king!* His face turned suddenly to one of deep consternation as he thought to himself, *What then shall become of me? And what shall become of my kingdom?*

> ### 1 Samuel 18:5-9 (NIV)
> "Whatever Saul sent him to do, David did it so successfully
> that Saul gave him a high rank in the army.
> This pleased all the people and Saul's officers as well.
> When the men were returning home after
> David had killed the Philistine, the women came out
> from all the towns of Israel to meet King Saul
> with singing and dancing, with joyful songs
> and with tambourines and lutes.
> As they danced, they sang: 'Saul has slain his
> thousands, and David his ten of thousands.'
> Saul was very angry; this refrain galled him.
> 'They have credited David with tens of thousands,'
> he thought, 'but me with only thousands.
> What more can he get but the kingdom?'
> And from that time on Saul kept a jealous eye on David."

When Self Stays on the Throne

Over the course of time, we see the man, Saul, steadily progress downward from the earthly state of the flesh into the soulish level. He soon attracts the demonic, and finally and very tragically ends up in the lap of the witch of Endor, seeking her advice because he has lost his stance with God. Although he had ample and successive opportunities to change and turn from the direction he was taking over and over again, he hurled himself onward, consumed with a frenzied desire to satisfy the passions of his base nature. He was led impassioned by the false way. It is what the Bible calls false wisdom, that is thinking in keeping with the fleshly mind versus the mind of the Spirit. It is thinking that is totally void of the influence of the Spirit.

I am sure you have met people, even Christians who have major issues with jealousy, envy, and strife. These enemies of righteousness seek to prey upon us all. The Bible says in James 3:16 that these vices lead to every evil work. It is only God's touch upon our hearts and minds that can bring us into transformation and healing. If, however, we refuse the gracious offer of God time and time again, as Cain and Saul did, we will find ourselves traveling alone down the dusty dirty road of our own fallen human nature with the enemy of our souls parading alongside us madly rejoicing that another one of God's people lost their chance to overcome by Christ. Off to the trophy room of Satan we go. It is not easy to obey God, but it is never worth the price we pay going our own way.

Job 36:10-12 (NKJV)
"He also opens their ear to instruction, and
commands that they turn from iniquity.
If they obey and serve Him, they shall spend their days
in prosperity, and their years in pleasures.
But if they do not obey, they shall perish by the sword,
and they shall die without knowledge."

Galatians 5:24-25 (Amplified Bible Classic Edition)
"And those who belong to Christ Jesus (the Messiah) have crucified the flesh
(the godless human nature) with its passions and appetites and desires.
If we live by the (Holy) Spirit, let us also walk by the Spirit.
(If by the Holy Spirit we have our life in God, let us go forward
walking in line, our conduct controlled by the Holy Spirit)."

Chapter Seven

Deliverance from False Wisdom

James 3:14-16 (NKJV)
"But if you have bitter envy and self-seeking in your hearts, do not boast and lie against the truth. This wisdom does not descend from above, but is earthly, sensual, and demonic. For where envy and self-seeking exist, confusion and every evil thing are there."

The scripture above is rich with some of the character traits that make up the personality profile of false wisdom. Let us look further into these mindsets mentioned in the above scripture and understand more fully the condition of the soul in the state of false wisdom. We can then get a better picture of what the scriptures say false wisdom is really like, how it manifests, and how to be delivered from it.

Bitter Envy

False wisdom is envious. Vines Expository speaks of envy as, *"The feeling of displeasure produced by witnessing or hearing of the advantage or prosperity of others."* It also says that, *"Envy desires to deprive another of what he has, whereas jealousy desires to have the same or same sort of thing for itself."* So we see that envy ventures down into a deeper notch of depravity than jealousy because it not only wants what the other has, but it wants the other person to be deprived of what is rightfully theirs. The word "bitter" in the above scripture, as in bitter envy, means that the person, on top of being envious, is very angry that the other person is prospering. Oh, the tragedy of our human hearts that remain untouched by God!

Self-Seeking

False wisdom devises plans and agendas that seek to promote self. Self-seeking is called selfish ambition in the scriptures. It is important to discern, both within ourselves and others: Is a person being propelled forward by the drive of selfish ambition or the quiet gentle leading of the Holy Spirit? When self is propelling a person, that person has to come up with clever manipulative ways to accomplish their goals in order to achieve their desires. On the other hand, when the Holy Spirit is doing the leading, one is not being driven but led and the flesh is in subjection. With the person that is led by the Holy Spirit, it is the will of God that is being pursued. For the one in selfish ambition, it is the will of self that is being pursued. Many are also deceived in this, intertwining the two somehow, believing that their will and God's will are one and the same. It is in these kinds of ways that we can deceive ourselves quite readily because of our drive for success, achievement, or some other personal gain or pleasure that has somehow become an idol in our lives. Idols, so often, remain hidden in our hearts. It takes a deep seeking of God and a great desire for truth to locate them. Many times the Bible sees our self-seeking agendas as lusting of the soul.

> ***Psalm 106:13-14 (Amplified)***
> *"But they hastily forgot His works; they did not [earnestly] wait for His plans [to develop] regarding them, but lusted exceedingly in the wilderness and tempted and tried to restrain God [with insistent desires] in the desert."*

Zeal often accompanies a person who is led by selfish ambition. But zeal without knowledge of God's ways, His time, and His order, leads a person to a very unproductive and negative result, not to mention the many heartaches involved. It is, therefore, wisdom to always stop and ask ourselves, would we rather have God or our self put us forward? I may add that self is always willing to take the helm and lead, but it requires great maturity and great meekness to abide under the disciplines of the Holy Spirit in this regard.

Only real soul searching and painful honesty will result in discerning the true motives of the heart. God can be "slow" in our estimation. We, therefore, can easily covet and manufacture faster, easier, less painful ways to get whatever it is we may want. Developing the fruit of the Spirit in our lives will prevent us from living a life of wasted efforts and foolish choices- none of which glorify God or are counted as righteousness in His sight.

In summary, until one really experiences what it is like when God opens a door, or when God truly leads, or when God says we are ready, we will be deceived in our Christian walk, thinking we are following God when in fact God is no where in our proximity, for we have charged on before. As long as self is on the throne, we will miss His way and forfeit our reward.

Boasting

With boasting, there are obviously issues of pride. Self is pushing itself forward and bragging loudly. Self is magnifying itself saying, "Notice me, Notice me!" With boasting, there is a distinct absence of humility. The word of God is clear about boasting. If we want to boast we may do so, but we may only boast in the Lord. We can brag on God all we want. Then we will be saying instead, "Notice the Lord! Notice the Lord!"

1 Corinthians 1:31 (NASB)
"... just as it is written, 'Let him who boasts, boast in the Lord' "

Confusion

Scripture clearly tells us that God is not the author of confusion (1 Corinthians 14:33). God is a God of order and peace. On the other hand, we can know that when confusion is in our midst, the enemy has entered into the situation. Satan loves disorder and chaos. This word "confusion" translates as disorder in the Greek. It is the sense of commotion. For example, the life of one in rebellion is a confused, mismanaged, disorderly life. People functioning by a spirit of rebellion are like mini tornadoes. You can tell when they have entered a situation because their "wind" disrupts everything and everyone in their midst. When they finally depart, it is amazing how quickly things come back to order and peace. This word "confusion" also means unstable, unsteady, and unsettled. Confusion uplifts everything from its secure resting place and tosses it in the air. Where there is confusion, we can know that false wisdom is at work and that the flow of God's Spirit is hindered and greatly diminished. In this state of mind, we are unsettled and unable to focus because we find ourselves within the whirling winds of disorder where nothing can be accomplished.

Jealousy, envy, and strife are precursors for confusion to enter in. I know when I step into a situation and sense confusion in the air that there is disunity of some kind, or there has been strife or competition at work. I recall a conference I attended where I volunteered to serve and in all the pre-conference meetings there was immense confusion. The Lord revealed that there was strife happening among the leaders and speakers. Satan had gotten in through strife, and it compromised the whole conference. Confusion and disorder were the result. Another time, I was overseas speaking at a small church and confusion took hold of me to such a strong degree that I could not speak on the subject God had given me to teach. I was embarrassed and excused myself. Later, I spoke to the Pastor, and he revealed to me that there had been a huge impasse between the leaders the night before. Again, I saw the power of strife to shut down the Holy Spirit and God's work. No wonder Satan wants us in jealousy, envy, and strife. Unfortunately, it is not hard for him most of the time to achieve his wicked ends.

Every Evil Thing

According to the scriptures, with false wisdom every evil thing is permitted to work. Why is this? It is because of all these traits: bitter envy, self-seeking, boasting, lying against the truth, and confusion are all attractive commodities to evil spirits. Moving in a consistent lifestyle with these mindsets and behaviors is like giving demons a work permit on site to set up camp and do their thing. This is why the scripture Jas. 3:16 concludes saying, " ... and every evil thing is there." Never underestimate the beginning indications of jealousy and envy. It is said of Saul that he *kept* a "jealous eye" on David. There is a difference in becoming jealous and letting it go eventually because it displeases God, versus "keeping" a jealous eye on someone. This meant that everything David did would be viewed through the filter of jealousy and envy. Mind you, it would not matter what David did - it was all now going to be seen through a veil of jealousy and envy. This is how this kind of thing works. Fleshly vices like these cause us to lose the right perspective and to take on an unholy bent that leads us down a false way. As we begin to pay attention to our thoughts and feelings and responses, we can catch these insidious attitudes that would destroy our intimacy with the Holy Spirit. When you perceive the green-eyed monster of jealousy rearing its ugly head in your mind, recognize it, own up to it, and crucify the flesh therein. The Holy Spirit will help you identify what is going on, and He will help you to not let that twinge of envy sink its roots into your mind and heart. May we all receive insight from God as to what is truly residing in our heart so we may repent and find God's ways and be free of these bondages.

> *Proverbs 4:23 (NLT)*
> *"Guard your heart above all else, for it determines the course of your life."*

Lying Against the Truth

> *James 3:14 (NKJV)*
> *"But if you have bitter envy and self-seeking in your hearts, do not boast and lie against the truth."*

Lying against the truth usually involves a refusal to look at sin or self. Though truth is pointed out, it is not embraced. Though the Holy Spirit is prodding us, we are ignoring the signals. A person can develop whole systems of operation that will serve to keep truth away. The backlash to this way of operating is that if we lie against the truth, we cannot be set free. Often times the beginning of any healing, restoration or deliverance is through a simple yet genuine admission of, you got it, the truth.

The most painful times in my walk have been when some ugly truth about my inner motive or the true state of my soul or heart was unveiled by the Holy Spirit, or by another person, or by a revealing circumstance of some kind that God allowed to happen. But the most wonderful and liberating of times in my walk have come through experiencing the incredible freedom and transformation of character that can only be realized by embracing the light of some needed truth that has been exposed. These are the deeper issues of life and the most meaningful ones. A person truly stands at the crossroads to make the decision whether to face truth and be changed, or to lie against the truth that is being revealed and thereby remain the same. Lying against the truth is denying or in some other way deflecting what is plainly being shown. This happens a lot, and it is the reason why many Christians do not grow or change.

Are You a Truth Avoider?

Lying against the truth, or to be in defiance of truth is a dangerous condition. For although the truth has been made evident and is seen and understood, it somehow is categorically denied. It is then that a further work has to take place to break down the walls, barriers, and obstacles of denial that serve to keep the truth away and out. I have discovered that there are four modes of denial that are always indications that truth is being resisted or denied:

1. Blame
2. Excuses
3. Deflection
4. Side-Stepping the Truth

Any of these or a combination therein can become a vice for avoiding truth. Are you a truth avoider?

I think we all are to a degree, but some are professionals at it. It takes real courage to look at truth. It is something that each believer must get used to because we are all being led intentionally by the Holy Spirit into all truth. If we avoid truth, then we will be avoiding the work of the Holy Spirit. If we avoid the work of the Holy Spirit, we will be avoiding necessary growth, and if we avoid necessary growth, then we will not mature and advance. Christ so desires for us to come into the truth and the light that we may be set free, but we often can instead be found hiding behind one or more of these denial modes and thereby hinder, delay, or permanently block our own freedom and release! Let us look at some of the ways we keep truth a safe and polite distance from ourselves.

1. A Truth Avoider through Blame:

We have heard it called the blame game. Blame is a way to deflect truth onto someone or something else. "It's not me, it's them!" Blame can be used by a person when they decide to refuse the truth. Blame can become a habitual knee jerk response to those who do not want to look at anything in themselves or be held accountable for anything - it's just easier to project the issue elsewhere. Adam and Eve took out the blame card and used it on God to relieve the pressure of confrontation. Aaron also played that card when called into account by Moses for letting the people run wild and worship a golden calf while he was gone up the mountain to seek God. As we mature, we can grow past this immature tendency that we all have fallen prey to at one time or another, or we can remain liars against the truth, as the scripture so states and never change, or own up to the truth when called upon to do so. The choice is always ours.

2. Truth Avoider through Excuses:

It is a fact that some people are excuse experts. It is a fear that if, God forbid, they tell the truth, they would be sentenced to a maximum security prison some where. It is not easy to admit and say, "I missed it," or "I blew it, and I am sorry." But how much nicer to honor the other with the plain truth than to give them some lame excuse. Excuses dishonor a relationship and the person to whom they are given, especially if it is an ongoing habitual act. Any hope of attaining a decent relationship with the person is forfeited because it is obvious many times to the recipient, that they are being fed something other than the truth. The game is up. Let us all just try telling the truth plain and simple and face the music. Initially it may be awkward, but at least there will be respect for being genuine.

3. Truth Avoider through Deflection:

Deflecting is in the same mode as the blamer, but it does not have a target in mind as the blamer does. In this case, there is no target. The truth is masterfully deflected. You just deflect over there some where and pretty soon you are on another topic. Wait a minute, how did that happen? Weren't we talking about this subject and now, somehow, we are talking about some other thing? Congratulations, you have just met the deflector. If they are really good, they can answer your question with an answer that doesn't have anything to do with the question. They will look at you with complete seriousness and make you wonder what *your* problem is! It is only as you walk away that you realize that you have just been had. This person will run you in circles. The best way to handle this dynamic is to constantly redirect the person back to the initial question. The truth is that the deflector needs some accountability, and perhaps the manipulative games will stop. Last thought, a deflector is always a manipulator.

4. Truth Avoider through Side-Stepping the Truth:

Once we see the truth of our sin then the Bible says we have to admit the truth. It has to come out of our mouths in the form of confession. This is God's way. "If we confess our sins, He is faithful and just to forgive us our sins and to cleanse us from all unrighteousness" (1 John 1:9). We have to hear ourselves say it. But even then, there is that unwillingness to completely come clean. I have been in corporate prayer sessions where the confession came forth as ... "Lord, if I have sinned, I am sorry," or "Lord, if I handled this wrong, please forgive me." One time in leading a prayer session at church, in a time of repentance and confession, I began to hear one right after the other succumb to this pattern of false confession. At the same time, there was a heaviness in the atmosphere as we continued to pray this way. Nothing seemed to lift it. Finally, I stopped the dull and lifeless prayer time by saying, "That's it! No more 'If I's' in our confessions. If we are saying 'If I' as a prefix to all our confessions then we are not squarely owning up to our issue, we are in fact side-stepping it. We are copping out, leaving it up to God to decide if we are at fault or not! It is time for us to own up to it. Did we or didn't we? No more 'If I's!' Then there was a long silence. It was pin drop quiet. Soon after, a Holy Spirit silence came upon us and brought us into a deep sense of His presence. Holiness entered the room. Then, a true spirit of repentance was manifested as people one by one, began to confess their sin openly before a holy God. No more "If I's!" No one was embarrassed, but each one of us was sacredly humble. We were at Bethel, and heaven had become open! Weeping and true repentance flooded in, and an awesome presence of God was ushered into our midst. We were truly forgiven and cleansed. Jesus was there. Oh my, what a time! No side-stepping here - just genuine repentance to a holy God. We were relating to God in truth directly. God desires nothing less. There are many ways we side-step truth but this unusual experience really highlighted the common tendency in us all.

Let us Become Truth Lovers

It is God's will that we become truth seekers and truth lovers. If we avoid every 'on ramp' that will take us into truth, we will miss our opportunity for advancement and freedom. Walking in truth takes courage. May the Lord help us all to become people of truth, full of integrity, walking in the light. We welcome You Holy Spirit, Spirit of Truth, please gently yet surely guide us into all truth.

Ephesians 4:15 (Amplified)
"Rather, let our lives lovingly express truth (in all things, speaking truly, dealing truly, living truly) ..."

3 John 4 (NKJV)
"I have no greater joy than to hear that my children walk in truth."

SECTION TWO

WISDOM FOR LIFE'S SITUATIONS

Chapter Eight

Wisdom for Fighting Fear

2 Timothy 1:7 (NKJV)
"For God has not given us a spirit of fear, but of power and of love and of a sound mind."

That Fear is not from God

In the above scripture, the Apostle Paul was exhorting Timothy to not succumb to a spirit of fear. Timothy was young, and he was starting out in the ministry. He may have had a youthful appearance that would initially give people the impression that he was not qualified or as experienced as he should be to hold such a position. Being young and "green" as some would call it, Timothy was ripe for the spirit of fear to come and hinder his call. But, Paul's words of wisdom on the subject of fear were: "God has not given us a spirit of fear," in other words, fear is not from God. And that is what God would say to you today, in whatever circumstance in which fear is coming against you, ... that fear is not from God.

Fear is a Spiritual Problem not an Emotional One

The other interesting thing regarding this scripture about fear is that Paul does not address this enemy called fear as a mere feeling, dealing then with aspects of our soul, but he gives us the added aspect that it is a spirit. He has said, "God has not given us a *spirit* of fear." So, he immediately locates for us the specific battle realm which is spiritual in nature and not of the soul. This does not mean that fear does not affect the soul, it just means that it's source and origin is from the realm of the spirit and the powers therein. So, in fighting the spirit of fear, we must understand that we are dealing with a spiritual force that affects our emotions, greatly but is not birthed or wrought from our emotional self. Why is this important? It is important because many people try to overcome their fear as though it were an emotional problem. But, I can tell you right now they will never solve it that way. This is because fear is a spiritual problem not an emotional one. Fear is of the realm of darkness and not of the kingdom of light. Therefore, the wisdom needed to solve it or deal with it has to be handled spiritually if you want to get to the root of an ongoing fear problem.

Fear comes from the outside of us to inhabit or dwell on the inside of us. It has to be received and taken in. If we conclude that fear is originating out of our own emotions, then we are saying that fear is a part of our self, but that cannot be true because God has not given it to us. The problem is that it affects our emotions and the feelings so intensely that we can mistakenly determine that it is originating from within our self. In truth, fear is not of you, and it is not of God. It is of the evil one. It has to be let in and received in order to work against you. We see this vividly when the Israelites were about to enter into the land of promise. They were all set to enter in. God was with them. He had let them know it's time to enter into the promise. He had given them His word. The spies went out to canvas the territory and came back with a fear report, and it swept through the camp attaching to all except Caleb and Joshua who did not let the spirit of fear come in. What was the thing that kept the fear from consuming them? They had God's word in them which by faith they believed. Their belief in what God had said to them was bigger than the fear that presented itself to them. But, the rest of Israel caved and received and took into themselves all that fear had to say. They completely disengaged themselves from what God had said. Fear was what they became married to and united with, so much so, that they threatened to stone Joshua and Caleb for speaking otherwise. The same thing happened when the serpent came to Eve. She received all that the serpent had to say and completely disengaged herself from what God had said. When we do these kinds of things at critical moments, at sacred turning points, we switch kingdoms and then for some amazingly stupid reason, we still expect God to be with us. Caleb cries out, "Only do not rebel against the Lord, nor fear the people of the land, for they are our bread; their protection has departed from them, and the Lord is with us. Do not fear them" (Numbers 14:9). But they sold out to the spirit of fear. Game over. Check mate. You can just pack it in and go home. The clincher? They were just a few short steps from gaining the long awaited promise of God. But they let fear come in and have its way unchecked. Lesson: If God has given you a word of promise, keep it, hold fast the confession of it, meditate on it so that no assignment of fear can displace it.

When Fear Tries to Minister to Us

When fear ministers to our mind, is there anything we can do? Yes there is, we can resist it. We resist fear by speaking the word of truth. Don't let your mind become occupied and consumed with thoughts of fear. We can resist these thoughts with scripture and fear will leave. Remember that fear is a spirit not an emotion, and God has not given it to us. Fear affects the emotions but it is not an emotion at it's foundation. Focus on what God has given us. The scripture says God has given us a spirit of love, of power, and a sound mind. You can resist fear by saying, *"Thank You Father that you have given me the spirit of love, the spirit of power, and of a sound mind."* In these ways we can begin to assert pressure through the agent of the Word of God against the forces of fear, and we can do this successfully through our belief and confession of His Word.

When Fear Comes in Waves

Another great scripture that the Holy Spirit supplied me in a time of fear was this one: "When I am afraid, I will trust in You." (Ps. 56:3) The reason this scripture worked so well for me was because it does not ask me to deny that fear. God was right there with me in that fear. When that fear narrative would start to rise up and gain momentum in my mind, I would state that scripture and literally turn those thoughts of fear directly over to God. Many times fear comes with a voice that tells you something terrible. Write down what fear is saying to you and resist those negative words with the Word of God. In my case, each time that fear would raise its ugly head, I would reject it saying, *"Lord I feel fear right now, but I am not receiving it, I roll these thoughts of fear and uncertainty over to You, and I place my trust in You."* Whatever your fear is, God is bigger than that fear. Since God is bigger you can certainly trust Him with it. Fear will come at times, but it's what we do with it when it comes that matters. And God's Word in this case says to roll it over onto Him and trust Him with it.

Governing Our Own Souls

God has given us the responsibility to govern our own souls. Scripture says that we are to guard our hearts with all diligence (Proverbs 4:23). We are to take every thought captive, making it obedient to Christ (2 Corinthians 10:5). We are to hide the Word in our heart (Psalm 119:11). It is our responsibility to do this. This is where our freedom is gained and our dominion is found. We are truly set free when we believe the truth and reject the lie. Let us not allow our feelings and emotions, induced by a spirit of fear, dictate its own reality and lead us along on its proverbial path of torment. The power to overcome in this life is found in one thing and that is the infallible unwavering truth of the Word of God. One way to begin to deal with an encounter of fear is to try and see Jesus standing in between that fear and yourself.

Let Jesus Become Our Shield

Psalm 28:7 (NKJV)
"The Lord is my strength and my shield; My heart trusted in Him, and I am helped;"

Sometimes, God will give us revelatory experiences to overcome issues that we face. In other words, He will give us a spiritual encounter to deal with the difficult issue. Isn't it nice to know that God will go to any length so that we can receive from Him and overcome? I will share a testimony with you that happened to me as a new believer. I was dreading a confrontation with a person who had been emotionally abusive to me for years. I had prayed that morning asking the Lord to be my shield because I was at the end of my ability to endure much more verbal abuse. I had come to the end. When a person lives under ongoing emotional abuse, being chipped away at day after day, their identity becomes stripped, weak, fragile, and shattered. Parts of myself were gone at this point, and I didn't know who I was anymore, and I was not sure if I even cared. I happened to read a scripture that morning which said, *"The Lord is a shield to all those who trust in Him" (2 Samuel 22:31).* It seemed to stand out from the page and beckon my attention. I meditated on it a while and went on into my day. I came home from work very tired and eventually, as was the custom, the moment came when the yelling started. I could feel myself being swallowed up in fear and defeat. The tears were about to start, and I would be driven into the same pathetic scenario, and then I said to the Lord under my breath, *"See Lord, here it happens again, I can't do this!"* All of a sudden, Jesus appeared standing right in front of me, between myself and the abuser. He was transparent yet visible! At once, the words that were taking me down for the count were no longer felt at all! All debilitating fear vanished and the harsh scathing words were being completely absorbed by Jesus. I felt nothing! I was amazed. Then the abusive words stopped and Jesus disappeared. There was a moment of stunned silence as I looked at the person. Then I spoke with an uncommon confidence and clarity to the abusive person and said, "I just want you to know that I don't receive any of that!" His face was one of great astonishment. He was taken back as if a pail of cold water was splashed into his face. He was strangely displaced, disorientated, and out of sorts because I had never responded like that before. I then turned and walked away. "Way to go Jesus!" I said under my breath. I was in awe that Jesus would stand up for me like that. I am telling you that we serve an awesome God! From that day forward, I had a revelation of a shielding Jesus. It is Jesus who will stand in between the enemy and ourselves. Jesus made His word come alive that day. He became what the word said He was - a shield. From then on, the Lord had me exercise faith against fear with Him standing between. By faith we can place Jesus between the fear and ourselves, and He will absorb the assault. He is indeed a shield to all those who trust in Him.

Developing a Strong and Courageous Spirit

Joshua 1:9 (NKJV)
"Have I not commanded you? Be strong and of good courage; do not be afraid, nor be dismayed, for the Lord your God is with you wherever you go."

It's every Christian's mandate from God to develop a strong and courageous spirit. It is necessary for us to acquire this strong and courageous spirit in order to advance spiritually and inherit the promises of God. In the book of Joshua, we find that Joshua is told by God that he needs two qualities that will enable him to possess the land. The two qualities are to be strong and of good courage. In the book of Ephesians, we are told a similar thing - We are told to, *"... be strong in the Lord and the power of His might" (Eph. 6:10)*. The Christian cannot dismiss these commands of the Lord and be victorious. They are the keys to overcoming. One of the things to remember about these commands is that God does not expect us to be strong in ourselves, but to be strong in the Lord.

The call to be a strong and courageous Christian is not merely a call to all the "spiritual warfare" Christians out there; it is instead the broad call to every child of God - no exceptions. The fact of the matter is, shrinking back is not pleasing to God, and its consequences can be devastating. The Israelites were intimidated by the giants in the land more than they were committed to standing by faith in the promise of God. They shrunk back from putting their faith in God, and instead chose to put their faith in the giants instead. This is why God left, I mean literally abandoned an entire generation to die in the desert. In our minds we know that God did that. But also, in our minds we think, *geez would God really do that?* Yep, He really did that!

Fear Cancels Faith. Faith Cancels Fear.

Fear's job, is to cancel and abort our faith. Faith is what births God's promises forth. Every victory in Christ must go through the birth canal of faith. If we allow fear to paralyze us from obeying God then the promise of God will be forfeited. One can almost hear the words when fear comes, "Abort! Abort!" Abort the stance, the assignment, the mission, the obedience. This is fear's job, that through chronic timidity, fear, and cowardice - we will be prevented from moving forward by faith into the promise of God.

But, as we base our faith on what God has said, we can anchor ourselves in a firm resolve of unmitigated truth. We can build ourselves up in our most holy faith by staying in the Word of God, meditating on it, and confessing it. The more we do this, the more likely we will recognize and dispel fear when it comes, and cancel it out.

Stepping Forward in Faith Believing

We insist many times that God take us out of the battle or around the combat zones of our difficult situations rather than through them. For those that insist on waiting for God to deliver them from the battle instead of taking them personally through the battle, they will be waiting a very long time because God doesn't do things that way. It is very much intended by God that we go through the battle versus being delivered out of it. Please receive this revelation because many are sitting on the sidelines of active passionate faith due to this mistaken passive stance. I remember one time I was in such a place, and when I finally decided to take some precarious steps forward, I suddenly felt God's engagement, His presence, and His distinct and precious anointing in the activity. I was surprised for I had been in a 'dry' place spiritually for a long time. In my heart, I said, *"Jesus, where have you been in my struggle in this situation?"*

"Waiting," He said.

"Well, I was waiting for You too Lord!"

With a sense of loving rebuke, and yet a distinct imparting of revelation He said to me,

"It is your faith that has engaged My presence and power, and this is the way it shall always be." I cratered. An unforgettable lesson. The truth is, we cannot go forward with Jesus except by faith. When we take faith steps, it automatically engages Jesus into our situation. Faith is never alone; it is always connected to Jesus. Faith is wonderful because Jesus is there. He is not there before you move out in faith, or while you are deciding to have faith. He is only there as you actively begin to move in faith. Our activation engages His presence. It is not something you pray about, it is something you do.

False Notions about Timidity, Cowardice, and Shrinking Back

One of the real pitfalls of timidity, cowardice, and shrinking back is this fallacy we hold to that somehow God is eternally sympathetic toward these fallen conditions of our soul. If we are not careful, we can place our timidity, cowardice, and shrinking back attitudes as a kind of "acceptable" reason as to why we cannot perform an obedience for

God. There is a misconception that, in God's great capacity for long-suffering, patience and mercy, that timidity, cowardice and shrinking back will forever be a valid reason for not moving forward in our walk with God. But, there comes a time when a prolonged unyielding stance of timidity, fear, and shrinking back are no longer considered as understandable as we may think it is. We cannot play the sympathy card forever. Maturation must occur. There comes a time when the Spirit of God will not strive with, bear with, or plead with us anymore. The balance of this truth is that there is most assuredly patience and abundant measures of grace and understanding with God regarding our personal issues of fear and timidity. But when we begin to use that stance of timidity as an excuse to not test the waters and move by faith, we can insult God. Holding back and shrinking away can actually be an affront to God. That means that it is an offense. He is very much grieved by it. Let's see this in the Word of God so that we can understand.

Hebrews 10:38 (New Catholic Bible)
"But my righteous one will live by faith. But if he shrinks back, I will not be pleased with him."

Amplified Version:
"... and if he draws back and shrinks in fear, My soul has no delight or pleasure in him."

We see the same kind of sense of this displeasure, rebuke, and disappointment from God in the man with the talents that hid them.

Matthew 25:24-26 (NASB)
"And the one also who had received the one talent came up and said, 'Master, I knew you to be a hard man, reaping where you did not sow and gathering where you gathered no seed And I was afraid, and went away and hid your talent in the ground. See, you have what is yours.'

> *But his master answered and said to him, 'You wicked, lazy slave, you knew that I reap where I did not sow and gather where I scattered no seed.'"*

The man with the talents said that he hid them because he was afraid. He gave the Lord back the talent when accountability time came. We must remember we will also have an accountability time coming with the Lord. In thinking about this man in the Parable of the Talents, we can say, it's not like he lost or squandered the talent or put it to bad use. He merely kept it under wraps and thought that it would be okay. Although he did not lose the talent, he didn't gain anything either. But the fact is, the Lord was fully expecting a return on the investment of the talent He had supplied. Apparently, being afraid was not a valid reason in God's sight. Let us note this, and rise up to God's viewpoint and not assume He has ours. God doesn't feel sorry for us because we are afraid, and therefore we are off the hook. He is wondering with all of heaven, why we are not working His Word and taking on the call to act in faith. Faith is where He shows up. Without it we are on our own. Who wants to be on their own when fear seeks to overcome us?

Face Off with Fear

It is the plan of God for every believer to be bold and courageous in the face of fear. I know we have heard it preached that even if we are afraid - to do it afraid. This is because there is something that happens when the believer decides to look fear in the face. It cannot be explained, it can only be experienced. The Spirit of God is powerfully engaged when we venture out to face the things we are called to face or to stand our ground where we have been called to stand - and not flee. It is in these times that we will sense His presence, and when we do we will then transition into the fullness of believing because we trusted in His word, and or obeyed His voice in that situation that required that we deal with that fear. We suddenly become conquerors of things we never thought we could conquer and victorious in situations where victory seemed hopeless.

> *Romans 8:37 (NASB)*
> *"But in all things, we overwhelmingly conquer through Him who loved us."*

Here's a brain-bender for you: we have already overcome. It is important to understand that we already have the victory because Satan was sorely defeated at the cross. He is ever hoping though that we will not really know this in mind and heart. The truth is, we are never fighting from a position of defeat or weakness, though we feel like it much of the time. The reality is that we are already raised up with Christ and seated with Him in the heavenly realms (Ephesians 2:6). As God said to the Israelites, the land is yours - now go, enter in and possess it! They had yet to possess it. God said it was theirs before they fought to overcome it. And that's where our faith fills in the blanks. We have it all by faith and we take it by faith and then fully possess it by faith. And fear can have no part of faith.

The Realm of Phobic Fear

The fact is I have had many fear issues in my life. Before I was saved, I was searching in many ways. I was seeking God by doing a lot of research and reading many books. On my night stand, I had books on New Age, Zen, the Zodiac, Jehovah's Witness, and Horoscopes, and I also decided that I should try the Bible and read that whole book through too. I reasoned that since the Bible was listed as a best seller for years that I might as well see what that was all about! So on my little night stand, I was inadvertently creating a huge amount of warfare of spiritual powers. I had no idea. It was not long after this that I developed a phobia. It seemed so strange that this would become part of my life. I consider myself a somewhat intelligent rational person, but I had somehow developed an inordinate fear of sailing. Now, this makes no sense since I grew up on the waters of the Long Island Sound, and used to spend many summers sailing out there. So here I was sailing my boat on Lake Travis in Austin, Texas as I had done many times before, and all of a sudden I began to become afraid. Very afraid. I started to hear haunting voices speaking to me in my mind telling me they were going to kill me. I would break out in hives all over my skin and feel rushes of coldness. This very real tangible fear and sheer dread would overcome me, and I would end up having to go back to shore. Then it would all subside. It made no sense. Phobias never do. So, I just eventually avoided the water all together.

I decided reluctantly to go to a psychologist to try to get some help with this. I couldn't believe this situation escalated to this point but I just decided to pay the money and go. I sat there and told him about this ridiculous irrational fear. His only explanation was for me not to feel crazy, that he had a lady in the week before who had a fear of feathers. I think he was trying to comfort me. He then explained softly and carefully how we would approach my fear. His solution was that we would take little outings in a small row boat and that he would patiently talk me through the issue first in the shallow water and then we would eventually approach the deep water. It was like I was a child or something. I thought to myself, *this is ludicrous!* And as he was telling me this, I began to hear the demons in my head laughing. They laughed and laughed and laughed!!! They would say, "We have you forever, and you will never be free!" And they roared hilariously. I thought, *They are right; this man, with all his medical degrees, has not a clue in a million of what I am dealing with!* Let me tell you that it was then that fear really came, forget the boat and all that, the real fear came when I realized that the medical world had not a clue about the kind of intense fear this actually was! The fear was not a medical issue but a spiritual issue. Then I knew I was alone, and I never felt so alone in my whole life. And those tormenting demons knew it. So I stopped going out to the lake. That's what phobias do; they cause people to work their life around their fear. The demons only seemed manifest out on the water, otherwise they were silent. It was the strangest thing. So, I just moved on.

The Door to this Fear was the Occult

If you have this kind of phobic fear with anything, then you need to know that it can only enter and become part of your life through the door of the occult or some kind of darkness. I had indeed opened a spiritual door of the wrong kind. I didn't know anything about this, but the dark side doesn't play fair. It banks on your ignorance. This is why the scripture says, *"My people are destroyed for lack of knowledge" (Hosea 4:6).* If people knew the Word of God and its power, these things would not happen. But I wasn't a Christian, and things like this were completely unknown to me. Eventually, I became a born-again believer and repented and renounced all occult associations; that is when the door of the occult became officially closed and that is when those demons of fear finally left my life.

Another Episode of Fear

Years later, I was plagued again by the same level of fear. This time it seemed that I could not sleep in my own house. I would go from room to room at night trying to not be afraid but it was not possible. Many sleepless nights ended up with me wandering the house, pillow and blanket in hand trying to find a place of peace and rest. I would hold the Bible over my chest and pray and pray and pray. Then I found a scripture that said, *"I sought the Lord, and He heard me, and delivered me from all my fears" (Ps. 34:4)* Every night I would pray and pray that scripture over and over. Many nights this continued. The only thing that brought sleep was if I went out into the driveway to sleep in my car. How strange is that? But it worked. I somehow could sleep in the car in my driveway but not in the house. I was too embarrassed to tell anyone about this. So, I just did what I had to do to deal with it. Do you know that the Lord sees every part of our lives? One Sunday, I was sitting in the church service and the Pastor interrupted his sermon and said, *"There is someone here who is experiencing fear to a great degree... and I am here to let you know that Jesus is going to deliver you, just follow His leading and you will be set free."* Well, I knew that I knew that it was me!!! Could it be? Yes, I knew it was! So sure enough, the night came and there I was with the fear starting up. Then I heard the Lord say, *"Go into the back room and look in the top file cabinet."* So, I did, and there I found a personalized astrological chart of my roommate's life! It was a reading from a person in the occult mapping out their life! The Lord told me to take it outside and to burn it. I really had not had any experience with deliverance, but I obeyed what the Lord said. From that night on, I was free. This is because, *"I sought the Lord, and He heard me, and delivered me from all my fears" (Psalm 34:4)*. God did just what His word said! He delivered me from all my fears. It was amazing. God does not want us to live in fear, and as we seek Him earnestly He will create a path for our deliverance.

Chapter Nine

Wisdom for Dealing with Guilt

Led By Guilt Pangs

In seeking God as to why I made some poor decisions in my past, He impressed upon me that many of the decisions and choices I had made were made because I was being led by guilt. As God began to work on this area, I felt as though He was rolling a threshing sledge over me and breaking open and breaking down the essence of how guilt-based decisions had worked so destructively in my life. We all know that we are under construction as Christians much of the time. Regarding this issue, God really had to tear up, and then renovate my mind as to how to live my life in a more constructive and productive way. It was a season where the Lord helped me become happier through finally being able to make confident choices based on truth and obedience to Him, versus making choices provoked by guilt and the fear of man. The Lord somehow worked change in me and gave me the ability to cut through to the black and white of things, instead of fumbling around in revolving cycles of emotional turmoil to make a decision. All the struggle and wrenching are now gone. It is a miserable bondage to be led by guilt pangs all the time. I am so much more content living more truly and sincerely to myself and others than I used to. I had false ideas about how to manage and govern my decisions, and the Lord began to clean it all up. Here is some of the wisdom He showed me.

Guilt By Way of Obligation

Learning to say no can be a hard thing for some of us. We grow up being trained to be polite and accommodating. We want to please and to have the approval of others. But if this need is out of balance, we will get ourselves into sticky situations by saying yes when we really want and need to say no, and saying no when we really want and need to say yes. When we feel an obligation (through ourselves or from another) to respond in a way that is always pleasing to others and never ourselves we are setting ourselves up for an abuse-based or victim-based lifestyle - a life of unnecessary relentless obligation. I used to get myself into all sorts of sticky situations with others because, through the fear of man, and also the need for approval, I would inevitably say yes to do everything. Over time, I found that I was stuck in a cycle of bondage. If I said yes and did what I did not want to do or need to do I would become angry, resentful, and pouty. On the other hand, when I'd say, "No, I'd rather not," I would have these guilt pangs and episodes of anxiety that I was not being very nice, helpful, or kind and that I was only thinking of myself. I would feel terrible and berate myself mercilessly for days. It seemed that no matter what answer I gave, I suffered a torment about it. As I brought it to the Lord, He began to speak a scripture to me.

Matthew 5:37 (BSB)
"Simply let your Yes be Yes and your No, No.
Anything more comes from the evil one."

The Lord was showing me several things. One, that it was okay to say no. I knew this in my mind but it was harder to play it out in real life. But the Lord was saying that if He was saying to say no, that I needed to obey Him and say no. He also was saying that I had come into bondage by not abiding by my own inner conviction. In fact, that one little word "no," was ruining my life not to mention my peace. But, as I allowed the power of this scripture to take hold in my life, not tossing back and forth by the bonds of guilty feelings every time

I seemed to disappoint somebody with a no, it began to take hold and I got free. I realized that I was coming into a deliverance. I studied about the times Jesus said no. He just said no and stuck to His plan which was the will of the Father. I believe the biggest no Jesus ever said was when he decided to hang back and not go and minister to Lazarus when he was deathly ill. He took the flack for that and then eventually, all those who complained saw the great wisdom of His firm and unequivocal no. When we compromise ourselves and God's will to appease a person because we are afraid of their reaction, we are in a place where we fear man more than we fear God. I clearly was not putting God in the highest place. On top of that, the word of God says that the fear of man will bring certain bondage.

A God Pleaser Versus a Man Pleaser

Proverbs 29:25 (NASB 1995)
"The fear of man brings a snare. But he who
trusts in the Lord will be exalted."

Well, I knew I was in a bondage cycle, no one had to tell me that. So, I decided to change because I noticed in the above scripture that God had promotion and reward for those who, instead of fearing man, put their trust in Him. As I did this, God began to prosper me and in the long run, I gained more respect from people. I realized what a sap I had been! I wasn't being as nice like I thought I was. I had been giving myself away and putting myself under man and out from under God's covering. As we learn to become God pleasers versus man pleasers, we will get it right and come out from under the wrestlings of our guilt-based battles.

Guilt By Way of Emotional Manipulation

Guilt can come from a variety of sources. If we have a controlling person in our life then many times that controlling person knows how to make us feel guilty in order to cause us to comply with their wishes. A controlling person can be an expert in dispensing guilt, making claims that if you don't do the thing they want you to do, that you will, "ruin everything for everybody." It is awful to live under these kinds of domineering personalities. It is a catch twenty-two in the sense that complying with the controller violates our free will, and not complying with the controller creates World War Three, especially when you are dealing with a Jezebel spirit. Usually, we just go for the false peace and succumb to the controller. But once that controller knows we can be had, it becomes harder to establish our right to say no. To make things worse, sometimes if the controller is a Christian, they will throw God into the mix and say that God is telling them to tell you to do such and such. Now we have a real battle going. The wisdom needed in this case is to simply know if God is telling *you* to do that thing. If not, then don't be pulled or pushed soulishly by an overbearing insistent person as this is nothing more than manipulation and pure witchcraft.

Avoid Yielding to the Voice of Intimidation

Another common sinkhole one can fall into is being intimidated into thinking that the controller is more 'spiritual' than us and can hear God more accurately than we do. We can easily be pulled under controlling spirits in this way. But God speaks to every single one of His sheep. His sheep do hear His voice (John 10:4). Therefore, if God is not telling you to do something, then don't do it. Some of us have developed skills in handling this kind of situation and others of us have not. The only way to combat this kind of manipulative guilt game is to know what God is telling you to do and do it. This is the bottom line though: we can be either victims or victors in Christ. We become victors through learning to hear God's voice for ourselves. This comes from being students of His Word. God does speak to each of us, so never let another one step in between you and God to hear for you what you should be hearing for yourself.

Guilt by Way of Condemnation and the Religious Spirit

As life would have it, there are those whom we come into contact with from time to time who feel, somewhat passionately I might add, that it is their calling in life, to fault-find, criticize, and condemn. In the church, it manifests as a religious spirit. The religious spirit has a fault-finding eye. It sees everything and everyone in terms of what they are doing wrong. Therefore, we need to be aware of the religious spirit imposing its condemnation upon us, making us feel guilty and condemned. We need to learn the difference between the Holy Spirit Who can, at times, zero in on a sin but Who corrects us with conviction and not condemnation. The religious spirit, on the other hand, will create a cloud of guilt over a person and cause a person to feel terrible about themselves. The religious spirit creates a sin-consciousness that is just not how Christ wants us to think or live. The scripture clearly states, "There is therefore now no condemnation to those who are in Christ Jesus, who do not walk according to the flesh, but according to the Spirit. For the law of the Spirit of life in Christ Jesus has made me free from the law of sin and death" (Romans 8:1-2).

Those led of a religious spirit also have a hard time ever admitting anything could be wrong with them, but they have an international ministry when it comes to sighting the faults and weaknesses of others! They interrupt, they insist, they point the finger, they live to litigate and intimidate. They are extremely insistent about their views, seeking to control and dominate others because they are convinced, without a shadow of a doubt, that they are right and you are wrong. If you see these qualities then I would say that this kind of fruit is certainly not of the Holy Spirit. Coming under the influence and power of a religious spirit will make you feel really guilty and condemned. Where do these strong guilt impressions and feelings come from? They come from those who are forming judgments and accusations against you by a religious spirit. These spirits are so strong that they will make you want to confess sin when you have no need to confess any sins. So, we can test the spirit of religion that may be working against us with this scripture.

Romans 8:31-34 (NKJV)
"What then shall we say to these things? If God
is for us, who can be against us?
He who did not spare His own Son, but delivered Him up for us all,
how shall He not with Him also freely give us all things?
Who shall bring a charge against God's elect? It is God who justifies.
Who is he who condemns?

After attending a conference I was home unpacking and I began to feel very guilty and condemned but could not think of anything that I had done that was wrong. The feelings of condemnation seemed to take over my mind. These negative feelings continued to come in waves over the next few days. As I sought the Lord He led me to this scripture, (Ro. 8:31-34 listed above), and I knew God was speaking to me. It made such an impression on me that I spoke it out loud. My mouth all of a sudden said afterwards, "The charges are dropped in Jesus name!" It was the Holy Spirit speaking through me to me! Then, I felt a huge break and a clearing in the spirit. Those awful feelings of guilt and torment left me immediately! I then had the sudden awareness that I had been judged and condemned by someone or several people. The Lord let me know that it was a religious spirit. So God delivered me from the ravages of the condemnatory nature of those who walk by a religious spirit. This great scripture was used as a tool of deliverance to combat the attack of condemnations through a religious spirit that came so strongly against me. This scripture freed me from the allegations, false charges and "guilty verdicts" that were in motion against me and are hallmarks of the religious spirit.

The Religious Spirit Seeks to Imprison Us

When there are standing judgments against us, especially through a religious spirit, it can be as if the case against us has already been tried, the verdict issued, and we have been somehow sentenced to prison. Judgments and condemnations are very powerful in the spirit realm. As I continued to seek the Lord that day, I also felt led to pray for the opening of a prison door that would free me from the 'prison place' of judgments that had been imposed upon me. This was to be the second half of the deliverance God was affording me.

Isaiah 61:1 (NKJV)
"To proclaim liberty to the captives, and the opening of the prison to those who are bound;"

So now I felt that I was to literally 'proclaim this liberty' and to also proclaim the 'opening of the prison unto which I had been bound.' And so I made that proclamation out loud. As soon as I did, I felt a huge break in the spirit, and a great sense of relief and freedom came to me. I was back in my right mind! We must not underestimate the power that religious spirits can carry. After all, it is the same spirit that killed Christ. It flows quite rampantly in the church, and it works to create disunity, to spread lies, and seeks most of all to kill the anointing. God wills that we not be subject to it. If I had not sought the Lord over those sweeping feelings of guilt and condemnation, those feelings would have remained on me and eventually would have effected me in a very negative way. But God imparted the needed revelation for me to get free, and He desires that all His children gain that same liberty.

Galatians 5:1 (NASB)
"It was for freedom that Christ set us free; therefore, keep standing firm and do not be subject again to a yoke of slavery."

2 Corinthians 3:17 (Amplified)
"Now the Lord is the Spirit, and where the Spirit of the Lord is, there is liberty [emancipation from bondage, true freedom]."

The Holy Work of Conviction

The Holy Spirit is given responsibility over us regarding the issue of sin. He is not called upon to *condemn* us for our sins and make us feel guilty. He is instead called upon by God to *convict* us of our sins so that fellowship and right standing with God can remain in place. Conviction is the warning button that the Holy Spirit pushes so that we can see that we have missed the way. This is not intended to condemn us but to cause us to re-align ourselves with Christ and His Word.

The Holy Spirit Knows How to Locate Our Sin

If there is something wrong with our life, the believer need not worry, God will let us know it. The Holy Spirit will manifest this to us in the form of conviction. He will let us know what is wrong, and He will speak to us in many ways to convey this. One such way the Holy Spirit lets us know something is wrong is through the sense of a burdened heaviness that does not lift, or through circumstances that come against us that somehow relate to our sin. He can speak to us in our prayer or our study time in the Word of God. He can speak to us through a dream, a vision, or through people, or anything else that will send a clear message to us that something is wrong and that we need to confess our sin and repent. The Holy Spirit knows how to locate our sin area. We can be sitting and listening to a sermon and all of a sudden, we may sense the preacher is speaking right to us about our problem area! What is this? This is the Holy Spirit locating our sin so that we can become aware that it is there and that it needs our attention.

The Conviction of the Holy Spirit

John 16:8 (NKJV)
"And when He has come, He will convict the world of sin, and of righteousness, and of judgment."

> *Psalm 32:3-5 (NKJV)*
> *"When I kept silent, my bones grew old through*
> *my groaning all the day long.*
> *For day and night Your hand was heavy upon me;*
> *my vitality was turned into the drought of summer. Selah*
> *I acknowledged my sin to You, and my iniquity I have not hidden.*
> *I said, 'I will confess my transgressions to the LORD,'*
> *and You forgave the iniquity of my sin. " Selah*

Experience has taught me that the more serious the sin issue is, the stronger the signal from God. The Holy Spirit has an uncanny way of hovering upon the area of sin, sort of like a helicopter circling over the sight of a crime. The Holy Spirit can bear down in a way that will surely let us know that He is present with His convicting power. The Holy Spirit will also pursue us to get things right because He knows that further down the road are real problems if we do not pay heed now! We may not think something is that important, but if the Holy Spirit keeps bringing it up, it is important! What God says is important. If we disregard the prompting and certain repeated convictions by the Holy Spirit and continue on the same faulty course, we will know in time, by the fruit of our life choices, that we missed the right way. Many times we learn the right way the hard way. The hard way can be called, The School of Hard Knocks. I have learned that it is better to graduate from The School of the Holy Spirit than The School of Hard Knocks! In any case, we will know in retrospect that it is the Holy Spirit who is trying to lead and guide us in the right way. The Holy Spirit knows the path that we are to take. He cares about our lives and deeply desires that we make good choices so that we can fulfill all the will of God our Father. It is always wisdom to yield to the Holy Spirit.

Knowing Who We are in Christ

The best way to combat false guilt attacks is to know who we are in Christ. If we do not know who we are in Christ then other people will tell you who you are. If you have an abuser in your life then that abuser will tell you who you are and why. If you have a controller or an intimidator in your life then they will tell you who you are and why. These kinds of people will have all the reasons and justifications as to why you are what they proclaim you are. But you, beloved believer, must know who you are in Christ. This comes from reading, understanding, and believing the Word of God and what it says about you.

Just Who do You Think You Are?

One day as a very young believer in an abusive situation, I was feeling very bad about myself and God asked me, "So who do *you* say you are? Are you who I say you are, or are you who they say you are?" God wanted me to choose. I had to decide who I was going to believe, God or "them." The wisdom that God was trying to teach me was, if I do not define myself someone else will. This is how victims become victims and remain victims. If you never define who you are, someone else has an image waiting for you to wear. If you never take on an identity, then someone else will come and brand you with one. But I chose that day to decide to learn about all of who I was in Christ. This, my friend, is what we need to lay hold of. Put on what God has fashioned you to be and who He says you are. God has a new person for you to step into today, it is called the new man (Colossians 3). No one is guilty in the new man. No one is under the law in the new man. No one is condemned in the new man. No, not even you, beloved believer.

Chapter Ten

Wisdom Regarding our Emotions

Emotions are a Faulty Foundation

It is a painful thing to have been led by the emotional self, believing with all your heart that you were going the right way only to find out in the end the fruit produced only loss, pain, and failure. I remember a wise teacher in school when I was a teenager trying to explain to me that love was not a feeling. She kept asking me what I thought love was, and I would blurt out... *"Love is a feeling that..."* And she would correct me and say, *"No, love is not a feeling."* Feelings to me were proof that my heart was wholly engaged and responding to the thing that I was feeling emotional about. Feelings were my proof that whatever I was feeling was real. But she was trying to cause me to see a greater wisdom - that real love was a decision of the will more than it was a feeling of the heart. Love certainly affects the emotions, but true love is founded and anchored in the will. This kind of love is committed because of the careful determined decision made by the person who is choosing to love. It is enduring and full of integrity. True love is not, on the other hand, the sudden and successive elevation of feelings accompanied by waves of wonderful emotions brought on by the emotional self. I mean if we think about it, which love would you rather be loved by? I think we all would say we would rather be loved by the love that is of the act of the will and not on a wild whim of the emotional self.

Beware of Emotional Decisions

The fact of the matter is, emotional decisions will ruin your life. I don't care how real they feel or to what degree we feel them, they are never the gauge we should use to make a decision. It is not without reason that many attorneys, counselors, and other professional people who are trying to help their clients advise: If you are going through a trauma or a significant loss of some kind, do not make a major life decision for at least six months. Why is this? This is because we are seeing everything in terms of our emotions at that time and not by an objective mindset. When we allow our emotions to govern our life, they can be the catalyst toward our downfall. I can think of no faster way to set a life off course than to be led by one's emotions. The dumbest and the most regretful decisions I have ever made were made because I allowed myself to be led by my feelings and emotions. To master the emotional self with its passionate feelings and powerful desires takes a certain maturity and is an acquired discipline. You can't teach this to someone. A person has to come to the knowledge of it, and many times that knowledge comes by pain. Some people never get a hold of their emotions placing them under the fruit of self-control, and for this reason their lives are mostly unstable and in a state of constant upheaval and disorder.

Emotions and Feelings Have a Place

Proverbs 29:11 (NKJV)
"A fool vents all his feelings, but a wise man holds them back."

Before we venture on, let me express here that God does not expect us to live our lives ignoring and negating our emotions, but He does want us to keep them in a proper perspective. God made us with emotions as part of our soul, so it is a natural thing to express emotions, feel emotions, and experience our emotions. It is important though to govern our emotions, but this is not to be interpreted to mean that a person would be advised to stifle and suppress their emotional self in order to be balanced. God does not intend that we stuff our emotions in a closet somewhere. He certainly does not wish that our emotions lay dormant and deadened to all feeling and expression. We can easily see this in scripture.

Romans 12:15 (NKJV)
"Rejoice with those who rejoice, and weep with those who weep."

Jesus was joyful at times and was also found weeping over the city of Jerusalem and cried also when Lazarus died. Jesus expressed open expressions of anger and passion as He went through His Father's house with a whip against the money changers. So emotions are surely to be felt and expressed. David obviously experienced great fervent emotion as he danced in freedom of expression in a loin cloth praising God, and this was to God's great delight! So, let us understand the difference between expressing our emotions in life's varied circumstances versus allowing our emotions to take the lead and to be the governing influence when we need to make a decision. There is a big difference.

Three Important Truths about Emotions

1.) Emotions are Unpredictable.

The problem with being led by our emotions and feelings is that they are fickle. They are up one day and down the next. Many people live on the roller coaster ride of their emotions, never getting off the ride to see more objectively where their course is taking them. The thrill of the ride is there, but it is not taking them anywhere; they are simply on a ride. Emotions are, in fact, the most unstable and unreliable part of yourself. Yet many people are in worship of their emotions. They are in love with the feelings and thrills and all the drama emotions provide them. They insist that their emotions are the validation for their choices and decisions. But a life led by emotions will soon begin to reflect just what the emotions are - flighty, unstable, and unpredictable. Most importantly we need to be led of the Holy Spirit, and to make our choices according to the will of God. He is the stabilizer that will keep us balanced and healthy in the area of our soul.

2.) Emotions are Deceptive.

Feelings and emotions are powerful. There's no doubt about it. They seem to convince us that they are the truth and the only truth. I know people who swear by their emotions. I used to. When we make our emotions the all-telling sign of unmitigated truth, we put them in an exalted place. But wisdom soon speaks through the sorrows of life that emotions are not the all-knowing truth that we once thought they were. Pretty soon, the feelings that were so real and convincing are no longer there, and we are left with the bad consequences of a poor decision. We thought the feelings were the proof, but alas, they were fleeting and momentary, clouding the truth, masquerading as the truth, and hiding from us the face of wisdom.

3.) Emotions Can Wreck Your Life.

It was the unchecked emotional state of anger that caused Moses to be denied access into the promised land by God. What a huge huge price to pay for the momentary thrill of expressing something he felt so deeply. It was David's feelings and passions that rose up as he gazed upon the beautiful Bathsheba whereupon he became impassioned to lay with her. Heavy prices to pay for allowing our feelings to have the best of us.

Called to Bring Discipline to our Soul

As believers we are called to bring discipline to our soul. The soul is comprised of the mind, the will and the emotions. When Jesus is asked into our heart to be Lord of our lives, many of us do not realize how extensive His Lordship is. Jesus is to be Lord over our mind, our will, and our emotions. To be Lord is to be a ruling force over.

Another way of saying this is that each facet of our soul is called to sanctification. Sanctification means that we are separated out unto the purposes of God. This means that our mind is called to come under the purpose and rulership of God, our will is called to come under the purpose and rulership of God, and our emotions are called to come under the purpose and rulership of God. And the Lord is wholly committed to this work in our lives. It is the work of making us holy. It is the work whereby we are sanctified. In fact, one of the names of God is, Jehovah Mekoddishkem - The Lord Who Sanctifies You (Exodus 31:13).

1 Thessalonians 5:23 (NKJV)
"Now may the God of peace Himself sanctify you completely; and may your whole spirit, soul, and body be preserved blameless at the coming of our Lord Jesus Christ."

This is the direction God is taking the believer in and the process is perfected as we yield ourselves to the leading of the Holy Spirit. As we yield, we are empowered to change and be changed. When we refuse to yield, the Spirit is grieved and the Lord steps back, (He is a gentleman), and we get to learn through life's lessons. I have learned, the hard way, that it is just better to yield to the Spirit, die to the flesh, and agree to His will - it saves a lot of heartache.

How Does God Seek to Rule through My Mind?

God seeks to rule through our mind by something called the renewed mind. It is the new mind of the new man. The renewed mind sees everything from God's perspective. The renewed mind understands and perceives God's will. If you want to know God's will then it will be found in the renewed mind. In fact, God's will can only be discerned in, what the Bible calls, the renewed mind.

The Renewed and Transformed Mind

Romans 12:1-2 (NKJV)
*"I beseech you therefore, brethren, by the mercies
of God, that you present your bodies
a living sacrifice, holy, acceptable to God, which is your
reasonable service. And do not be conformed to this world, but
be transformed by the renewing of your mind, that you may
prove what is that good and acceptable and perfect will of God."*

Every Good Decision is Made in the Renewed Mind

The renewed mind is the mind that is refreshed and made alive in Christ. Many times we experience the condition of the renewed mind after church on Sundays. We may come to church weary and tired, frustrated or worried, perhaps depressed or angry or indifferent. But when we leave after being in the presence of God and after sitting under the anointed preaching and teaching of the Word, we become changed somehow. This, my friend, is the renewing of the mind. Now, in the renewed mind, we see more clearly, now we have peace and joy even though our circumstances may not have changed. It is essential that we keep ourselves, continually refreshed in the renewed mind that the Bible talks about. It is only in this state that we should make our decisions. Bad decisions, wrong thinking, and negative attitudes are part of the mind-set that is in the flesh mode. We need to know when we have reverted back to the old self and the old mind so that we can catch ourselves and immediately do what is necessary to get back into the new self, that is renewed in knowledge after the image of Him Who created him (Col. 3:10).

Romans 8:5-6 (NKJV)
*"For those who live according to the flesh set
their minds on the things of the flesh,
but those who live according to the Spirit, the things of the Spirit.
For to be carnally minded is death, but to be
spiritually minded is life and peace."*

How Does God Seek to Rule in My Will?

Many times, we experience the battle of our will versus God's will. When the believer yields his or her will over to God in a certain area of his or her life, the Holy Spirit then takes action to provide the enabling power within the person, to accomplish God's perfect will in that situation. As we learn to trust God, we will begin to yield ourselves more fully and freely to Him. We then soon find out through many experiences, that the things we have yielded to God have resulted in us benefiting and being blessed in many ways. It is then that we are able to turn over more and more of ourselves and lives to Him because we come to understand that it is always God's will to better our lives in some way.

Psalm 143:10 (NKJV)
"Teach me to do Your will, for You are my God; Your Spirit is good. Lead me in the land of uprightness."

How Does God Seek to Rule in my Emotions?

The person who has control over their emotional self has come into maturity. We can look at children and see the wide range of emotions that they exhibit from one minute to the next. They are children expressing the fullness of everything they feel and want and desire. But a weaned child is different. A weaned child participates with the parent to become more mature. A baby needs to be weaned off the bottle eventually. A child needs to be weaned off of sucking their thumb eventually. And so, the process goes. Well, as Christians, we are expected to allow God to wean us off our flesh too, or we will remain babies in the spirit instead of coming into the fullness of maturation and adulthood that God desires. Unfortunately, this can be the state of many Christians who are living in carnality yet calling themselves disciples of Christ.

The Weaning Process

So what is this process called *weaning* all about as far as the Christian is concerned? Webster's defines it for us:

To Wean: *To train, to withdraw by degrees from a habit or behavior. To detach the affections from something followed or desired.*

Weaning is not an abrupt change but a slow methodical and deliberate one. In the following passage of scripture the Psalmist perceives the work in his soul called weaning.

> ***Psalm 131:2 (Amplified)***
> *"Surely I have calmed and quieted my soul;*
> *like a weaned child with his mother, like a weaned child*
> *is my soul within me (ceased from fretting)."*

We see an interesting aspect of the discipline of the soul in this scripture. The Psalmist has taken it upon himself to calm and quiet his own soul. I believe this discipline was acquired over time. The desire and ability to step back and wean ourself off of impassioned emotions and feelings and to quiet and calm the soul before God is a mark of maturity in God's eyes. It is in this way that we take authority over our emotional self. We cannot live by the Spirit and live by the flesh at the same time. The flesh has to die. The ability to wean ourselves off of our fleshly feelings and emotions in certain situations is a needed commodity for life's many challenges. Part of wisdom is to know this and to participate in the process with the Holy Spirit leading the way. The Apostle Paul shares this concept with us quite beautifully in the following passage of scripture.

> ***1 Corinthians 13:11 (NKJV)***
> *"When I was a child, I spoke like a child, I understood as a child,*
> *I thought as a child; but when I became a*
> *man, I put away childish things."*

The Secret of Stilling the Soul

Stilling the soul is a spiritual discipline that will cause us to hear the voice of God more clearly. Emotions push and pull against this stilling, but the Holy Spirit eventually places us in perfect peace as we move in this direction. It is only when the soul is at peace that we can make a decision based on the wisdom of God. It is important also not to allow anyone or anything to push or pull you into a decision that affects your life before you have had time to be alone and to still your soul before God. Let us read the words of the Psalmist again about stilling of the soul. Notice that David says, "I have stilled and quieted my soul..." This is something *we* do, this is something that *we* take action on, as a spiritual discipline. The enemy of our souls would love to pull us out into our emotional self, and cause us to make a really bad choice or to be led in some way by strong emotion, and then be stuck to have to live with that bad choice and its various negative consequences.

Be Still and Know

I remember one of the most trying times in my life in which I was insistent that things had to be different and had to change. I was pleading with God to redirect things, to help me, to move in some incredible way to alleviate the problems of the circumstance. I was exasperated and anguished and my emotions were in full tilt, and then the Lord impressed my mind very clearly with the verse, "Be still, and know that I am God..." (Psalm 46:10). His counsel, in the midst of all the turmoil, was to be still and know that He was God. I already knew He was God, and I didn't want to be still! My flesh was screaming, and I was in utter dismay that, according to God, nothing was going to change for the time being! It was at this time that God was teaching me the secret power of stillness. I began to read the scripture, "Be still, and know that I am God," in the context of the whole Psalm. The message is a powerful one. Basically, it is this: I don't care what's going on around you and what has you so upset or worked up, I can provide you a place in Me that will keep you at peace in the midst of the storm.

Psalm 46:1-7 (NKJV)

*"God is our refuge and strength, a very present help in trouble.
Therefore, we will not fear, even though the earth be removed,
and though the mountains be carried into the midst of the sea;
though its waters roar and be troubled,
though the mountains shake with its swelling. Selah
There is a river whose streams shall make glad the city of God,
the holy place of the tabernacle of the Most High.
God is in the midst of her, she shall not be moved;
God shall help her, just at the break of dawn.
The nations raged, the kingdoms were moved;
He uttered His voice, the earth melted. The Lord of hosts is with us;
the God of Jacob is our refuge. Selah*

In these previous verses, I saw it. I saw myself in this storm where everything was shifting and changing and in crisis, but God was in the midst and I was not to be moved. I was to be still and know that He was God even in the middle of all that was shifting and shaking around me. Then the Psalmist says: "There is a river whose streams shall make glad the city of God, the holy place of the tabernacle of the Most High. God is in the midst of her, and she shall not be moved…" (vs. 4-5). What was God saying? God was saying to me, I don't care what outward circumstances are happening around you - there is a place in Me that you can find by stilling your soul. In fact, there is a river. It's an unknown untapped resource completely unknown to the world. It is there that you will find all the rest and strength and grace and joy and peace that you need - yes even in the storm.

God Has Hidden Reservoirs

It is interesting to know that there are those who believe that Jerusalem has a subterranean water supply that provides water to the city's many fountains and pools. Though unseen and hidden, the secret water supply serves as a perfect symbol of the inner grace and peace that only God can give. Much like this subterranean water supply in

Jerusalem is the ministry of the Holy Spirit inside the believer. The outer life may have many difficulties, whereby it looks like we would be found wanting and in dire need. But we need not fear, though hidden from sight in the subterranean level of our temple, there is a river whose streams shall make glad the city of God, the holy place of the tabernacle of the Most High. We are that tabernacle (1 Cor. 6:19). So now, what is it that you would rather have ministering to you, leading you, and influencing you in your life and your decisions? Is it the roller coaster ride of those feelings and emotions that your flesh is ever ready to provide you at any given time, or is it instead, that secret place of the stillness of the soul that has been calmed and quieted by you, and sustained by the indwelling of the Holy Spirit?

Chapter Eleven
Wisdom to Combat Intimidation

It's a Matter of Stepping Into Our Authority

1 Corinthians 16:13 (NKJV)
"Watch, stand fast in the faith, be brave, be strong."

I had been invited to speak at a conference. I was sitting next to my husband who leaned over to me right before I was introduced and said in my ear, "Step into your authority." Step into my authority? Why was he saying that? I briefly breathed a short prayer and went up to the podium to begin the message God had given me to speak. As I spoke a while, I came to notice a certain resistance in the atmosphere. I continued on to try and move past it, but it seemed as if my words were hitting an invisible wall and going no where. This was strange as I usually was able to engage the audience. As I scanned out among the people, my eyes suddenly were arrested on two people who were stone-faced with their arms crossed. It took me back a moment. I began to falter in my speech and then began to feel at a loss for words. I was all of a sudden intimidated. It was then that I heard my husband's words come back into my mind ... "Step into your authority." Stephen had heard from the Lord. He sensed that this message would be a battle for whatever reason. So, I pressed back into the message with more authority, repeating the words I had just spoken to further emphasize my point, and I kept holding the stance of authority of what God had told me to say. I also leaned into the podium to further push against this invisible barrier that was trying to block the message. I soon felt the resistance lessen and eventually, the intimidation broke off and there was a release in the atmosphere. The meeting from then on was unhindered and free. What broke, I soon learned, was the spirit of intimidation.

It is easy when intimidated to think there must be something wrong with us. But we must consider when we are beginning to feel intimidated that it may have nothing at all to do with us and everything to do with the other person or people. Intimidation wants to pull us down under its looming cloud of fear, but we must resist the onslaught and continue our mission - whatever it is. In another instance regarding the spirit of intimidation, I remember being told by my boss to take the meeting for her and relate the estimates to the client on a project. Sounded simple enough, but as it turned out, the man I met with was a tough cookie. He never spoke the whole time. When I would look up for a response of some kind to what I was presenting, he offered none. As I continued, I joked a little to try and lighten the mood, but there he was remaining fixed in the same silent seemingly uninterested frozen attitude. Soon, I began to feel that weird unsureness from within. I felt awkward and uncomfortable and yes, intimidated. But I caught it before it took me down any further. I knew I was doing just what I was supposed to be doing - relating the facts on a job proposal. I refused, in my mind, to be taken off my course. So, I gathered up some confidence and boldness and with firm resolve decided I had a message to deliver and, by golly, I was going to deliver it. I was at least going to do my part. If he wanted to exude some kind of power play persona by not speaking then so be it. I took control, spoke the facts, and left him with the ball in his court. I said, "We won't begin until we get a signature, and if we do not have a signed proposal by Friday, we will assume you are not interested in working with us. We will then move on to our next client. Thank you for your time," and I exited the room. Thus, taking the bull by the horns approach, was all that I could think of to do in a situation like this. In any case it worked. Intimidation failed to take hold of me. But it was a battle of sorts to work through. Here are some things to be aware of regarding the spirit of intimidation.

The Four Assignments of Intimidation:

1.) It is the Assignment of Intimidation to Displace us from our Vision and Purpose

Since the spirit of intimidation seeks to displace us from our vision and take us off course, it is important to have a resolve within ourselves about our mission. It is important to not allow anyone to interfere with our vision and purpose to the extent that we are distracted from completing it.

No Man Shall Stand Before You

Joshua 1:5 (NKJV)
"No man shall be able to stand before you all the days of your life; as I was with Moses, so I will be with you. I will not leave you nor forsake you."

God promises that no man shall stand before us but we are responsible as well for keeping ourselves on the path of our vision and purpose. When we slip off that path by means of becoming fearful and intimidated, we will not only forfeit the purpose and mission of what we are trying to accomplish, but lose the sense of God's presence and anointing to help us as well. Once we lose the sense of God's presence and the anointing it is all downhill from there.

Every great person of faith has had to wrestle through the warfare of keeping their vision in place. Make no mistake; it is a warfare. Nehemiah was a man with great vision and purpose, and the enemy made sure to try to thwart his progress repeatedly. How? Through the spirit of intimidation. People were repeatedly sent to Nehemiah to intimidate him out of his call to rebuild the wall. In all the various ploys of intimidation, (mocking, slandering, threatening among others) Nehemiah did not budge off the assignment God had for his life. He let no man stand before him in what God had called him to do. He is a wonderful example of someone who did not fold under the repeated, constant, relentless pressures of intimidation.

2.) It is the Assignment of Intimidation to Inspire and Control a Person through Fear

Psalm 118: 5-6 (NKJV)
"I called on the Lord in my distress; the Lord
answered me and set me in a broad place.
The Lord is on my side; I will not fear. What can man do to me?"

The spirit of intimidation longs to inspire and provoke a person to fear and insecurity. This kind of fear has a gripping effect upon the mind, which seeks to render one as inferior and incapable. It preys on a person's perceived weaknesses and seeks to locate apparent faults in order to render a person unstable. Once instability sets in, confusion hits the mind; its all downhill from there. There are several stages of how intimidation takes a person down. We can learn how to recognize the signs that intimidation is at work, and thereby quench it sooner than later. Here are the stages of intimidation:

a.) Fear and Intimidation: The attack begins with unexpected fear and unsureness

b.) Doubting: You start to slip off your original plan due to an unexpected, unfounded lack of confidence

c.) Confusion: You begin to doubt your message or assignment.

d.) Frustration: You know you had the vision and the resolve, but now you don't understand where it went. Sometimes we become angry at this point as well. This only exasperates the matter.

e.) Displacement: (You are now officially out of your anointing). You are in a ditch that you cannot raise yourself out of. You have lost your purpose.

This is the place Elijah found himself in when Jezebel threatened him. God's words to Elijah were, "What are you doing here, Elijah?" This is indicative of the reality that Elijah was completely displaced from his call and his spiritual position of authority.

f.) Defeat: We give up completely and throw in the towel. The enemy called intimidation has won the battle.

3.) It is the Assignment of Intimidation to Nullify Your Faith.

Psalm 56:3 (NKJV)
"Whenever I am afraid, I will trust in You."

The reason the enemy likes to use intimidation against the saints is because it is a faith paralyzer. You are going along fine but then intimidation comes and arrests your attention to destabilize you. Your focus becomes changed and the word, vision, or plan God originally gave you becomes difficult to discern and strangely displaced and perhaps even foreign to you. Why is this? This is because the spirit of intimidation has the power to dislocate our faith if we do not stand in our authority. So intimidation does not want to just make you afraid for fear's sake; it wants to make you afraid in order to block whatever it is you have been called to do. It has an assignment.

4.) It is the Assignment of Intimidation to Cause You to Fold Under Pressure

The way this spirit works is to increase pressure steadily and repeatedly until a person lets go of his or her authority and gives up. God does not want us to give in to intimidation. He wants us to stand in the face of it, stationed in the place He has called us to be, to do whatever it is He has called us to do. God will prepare, forewarn, train, and help us to overcome the spirit of intimidation. Let's look at how God prepared the prophet Ezekiel to stand in the face of intimidation.

I Have Made Your Face Strong

Ezekiel 3:8-9 (NKJV)
"Behold, I have made your face strong against their faces, and your forehead strong against their foreheads. Like adamant stone, harder than flint, I have made your forehead; do not be afraid of them, nor be dismayed at their looks, though they are a rebellious house."

God had a mission for Ezekiel and that mission was to speak to a rebellious people, but before God had Ezekiel speak to the people, he fashioned him for the task. The scripture above shows us this. In essence, to the degree that he would meet with resistance is the degree to which Ezekiel was fashioned to withstand that resistance. What God said to Ezekiel basically was that the people I am sending you to speak to are incredibly hardheaded. They have one way of thinking, and they are not budging. So, I, as God, have some things to say to these people even though they are exceptionally hard-headed, stubborn, and rebellious. I am going to send you, Ezekiel, as My messenger to speak to them. And to prepare you, I am going to make you just as hard-headed, but hard-headed with the truth. You are not to back down, condescend, or be moved. You are not to be afraid or timid. No shrinking back allowed. I want you to resist intimidation and to speak what I want said. When you are hit with that resistance, hit right back with the truth. Intimidation will try to displace and derail your mission, but I have fashioned you for this task and have called you to speak My words to these people. Aren't you glad you were not Ezekiel? It is interesting to note that Ezekiel's name means, 'strongly seized by God' or 'God strengthens.' Ezekiel was uniquely strengthened by God to face his intimidators. And, if you are ever called to face such levels of intimidation, God will strengthen you too.

Standing Against Intimidation

One of the most powerful warfare strategies for the believer is to stand. When we stand, we occupy a place in the spirit realm. When we fail to stand, we fail to occupy. When we fail to occupy, we forfeit the battle. There is an enemy who seeks to challenge us at every turn. We need to stand on the word that God has given us for the battle. Standing is a Christian's power tool against all the wiles and ploys of the enemy. Don't move off your spot. Stay planted, and you will soon see the salvation of the Lord.

2 Chronicles 20:17 (NKJV)
"You will not need to fight in this battle. Position yourselves, stand still, and see the salvation of the Lord, who is with you ..."

Chapter Twelve

Wisdom Concerning Flattery

Psalm 12:2 (NASB)
"They speak falsehood to one another; with flattering lips and with a double heart they speak."

Insincere Praise

Often times, we can be led along by people through the means of flattery. Flattery is a form of verbal manipulation. It is a way to get a person to do what you want them to do for the benefit of the flatterer. Flattery praises falsely in order to gain favor or an advantage in some way. Flattery compliments excessively and insincerely, in order to win over a person. Flattery also engages in speech that is as smooth as butter but is entirely insincere. Flatterers know how to make things sound so good and appealing. Flattery is also defined as a form of lying. Motives of self-interest always rest in the heart of a flatterer. When someone has resorted to flattery, they have set in motion a personal agenda, and certainly do not have your best interests at heart.

I remember a time when the Holy Spirit arrested me saying, "Their heart is not with you."

Resisting the thought I said,

"But Lord, they are so nice, and I don't think they would lie to me."

Yet again the Lord warned .... "Their heart is not with you."

Now disturbed and deeply disappointed, I thought, was this really true? That low dipping sinking feeling was fast becoming a queasy churning in the pit of my stomach. I was doing just fine; now the Holy Spirit was witnessing strongly in a way that was difficult to deal with. I could not ignore it. I had to face the truth of what the Holy Spirit was witnessing to me in my spirit. I was grieved and genuinely hurt to know this truth. As I continued through the situation, I could see by the light of God that it was true. I was then willing to let wisdom weave me through the particular circumstance carefully and safely. Seeking the Lord more diligently, He let me know that flattering speech was seeking to seduce me into decisions that would result in great loss to me and our ministry. How wonderful the Holy Spirit is Who leads us into all truth, as we take heed and listen to His voice and counsel.

Romans 16:17-18 (NIV)
"I urge you, brothers and sisters, to watch out for those who cause divisions and put obstacles in your way that are contrary to the teaching you have learned. Keep away from them. For such people are not serving the Lord Christ, but their own appetites. By smooth talk and flattery they deceive the minds of naive people."

Sugarcoated - Duly Noted

Wisdom says, if someone is laying it on thick and sugar-coating everything, something is up. The smooth talker, the slick Willie, the one who coaxes with compliments galore .... all these can be forms of flattery. If you are needy or emotionally starved, then you can be vulnerable to the voices of flattery, praise, and compliments. If you are seeking support or approval at a certain juncture in your life, you can be drawn into situations through flattery. Flattery appeals to our pride, our desire to succeed, our need to be liked and accepted. Flattery appeals to those areas in ourselves that maybe no one ever took the time to nurture or recognize. In these kinds of ways, flattery is cruel and wicked. It takes advantage of an innocent soul, or one who is naive and simple. Flattery hurts because it has been insincere and, at the same time, has sought to profit from one who is trusting, vulnerable and innocent. In conclusion, flattery ruins any chance of a good relationship because it has abused that privilege.

Proverbs 26:28 (NKJV)
"A lying tongue hates those who are crushed by it,
and a flattering mouth works ruin."

Come Out of Simplemindedness

We can put all the blame on the flatterer but the scriptures exhort us to not be so foolishly naive. The Bible speaks of the naive person as a simpleton. The term "simpleton" denotes a person who lacks wisdom from God. Proverbs says that, *"Only simpletons believe everything they're told! The prudent carefully consider their steps"* (Proverbs 14:15). Hence, we see that the simpleton needs to wise up and start using good judgment. One only needs a few encounters with the insincere praise of a flatterer before they begin to take on the wisdom of God. As we seek God regarding our relationships, He will show us the things we need to see so that we can avoid the trouble flattery can bring.

Flattery & Thievery

I've had my encounters with the nasty ways of flatterers as I am sure you may have as well. Here is one incident that remains burrowed in my memory. I was entertaining in my home with many people filling the rooms. Laughter and conversation were plentiful and the goodness of God was there. It was then that a person approached me, pulling me aside alone to speak. I did not particularly know her, and there she was batting her eyes and profusely complimenting my home, and so she continued to elaborate and compliment and praise all the things of the home in a way that did not make me feel right. In fact, I was somewhat uncomfortable. I knew something was up but I didn't know what. My rational mind pushed away what I thought was a bout of negative thinking. This woman was committed in conversation to arrest my attention and to compliment and praise in a way that was not appropriate to our relationship. It puzzled me, and because I could not think of why this could be occurring, I passed it off as a bubbly perhaps somewhat over-talkative nervous person with an exceptionally strong personality. Some time later, weeks after the party, I was inquiring of the Lord about thievery in regards to a ministry situation that I had become aware of. I prayed a prayer saying, "Lord if there is a thief in the house (of God) then let them be exposed so that Your house may be cleansed and righteousness be restored!"

And again I prayed,

"Lord reveal the thief in the house ..."

I prayed that prayer many times in the next few days. Then one night, I had a dream. It was a dream where I was being shown something. I was shown a certain person whom I knew and she was in my home stealing some silver from our dining room and placing it in her purse. It was as clear as day! At the same time, I knew the day that this happened. It was the day the over-talkative flattering lady (her partner in crime) had steered me away into another room to have that weird flattery-based conversation. I was astonished! My prayer to God had been,

"Lord, if there is a thief in the house please reveal it to me."

Though I was meaning His house - the church, God showed me my house!!! There is something to be said about praying prayers that ask the right questions! Sure enough, I looked in those drawers and my grandmother's silver spoons were gone. I hadn't had the need to look there in months. The next time I noticed this person at a meeting, she was carrying the same purse I saw in the dream the Lord had given me! Although this story is mainly about a theft, I wanted to relate about the woman who obviously was in agreement with the thief, who used the corrupted yet effective tool of flattery as a means to "capture" my attention long enough to effect the crime. This is an extreme case of flattery but my point is, flattery never has a good outcome. If someone is laying it on thick - get out and away from the conversation.

Needless to say, I was in a quandary as to what to do. What was taken could never be replaced as it was a family treasure. I grieved over the flagrant disregard for another's property and also for the kind intention of my grandmother who had given it specifically to me to enjoy and those in our family after me. Now it was lost forever. I chose to forgive them and release them. Beyond this I was led by the Lord to leave it alone. He told me that any confrontation would meet with a lie. God just wanted me to know. This situation made me understand in a keener way than ever before, that God really does see everything we do. It was like seeing film footage when He revealed it to me. It heightened my fear of the Lord and the coming Day of Judgment, when the books are opened and the secrets of men are revealed and laid bare (Revelation 20:12-13). It is true that we serve a God who reveals secrets (Daniel 2:28). He causes His servants to know things that could not otherwise be known except that we have prayed and He has revealed.

Flattery and the Spirit of Jezebel

Flattery is also one of the seductive tools of Jezebel. If Jezebel wants something (and she always does), then many times the person operating by a Jezebel spirit will compliment and praise the weak or needy area of a person. The Jezebel spirit has an uncanny way of locating those weak wanting areas of the soul. She coaxes her agenda along with candy-coated words of flattery knowing that the bait will eventually be taken. She then knows she is on her way, smoothing the path, honeying up the pot, so to speak, towards getting what she wants. Flattery works manipulation and seduction, two of Jezebel's most notable character traits.

Flattery and the Absalom Spirit

2 Samuel 15:2 (NASB)
"Absalom used to rise early and stand beside the way to the gate ..."

Absalom sat at the gate ready to meet (intercept) the needs of the people. He had an agenda in mind to usurp the throne of his father's kingdom. He did not do it with the skills and weaponry of a warrior. He did it by winning over the hearts of God's people, by taking an insincere self-motivated interest in them. His charm, his engaging personality, his uncommon niceness topped off with gobs of flattery accomplished what he was after - stealing the flock of God right out from under King David's nose. There were two kingdoms within the kingdom now, David's diminishing one and Absalom's increasing one. Absalom's ministry was not subject to David. The Absalom spirit presents itself as one of the most formidable powers that work against the unsuspecting people of God. Flattery, make no mistake, is always part of some kind of diabolical package.

It is interesting to see the opposite spirit at work in the Apostle Paul's ministry to the church in Thessalonica. The purity of motive cannot be mistaken. This is what the church should be all about.

1 Thessalonians 2:4-7 (NKJV)
*"But as we have been approved by God to be
entrusted with the gospel, even so we speak,
not as pleasing men, but God who tests our hearts.
For neither at any time did we use flattering words,
as you know, nor a cloak for covetousness -
God is witness. Nor did we seek glory from
men, either from you or from others,
when we might have made demands as apostles of Christ.
But we were gentle among you, just as a nursing
mother cherishes her own children."*

Flattering and Seducing Spirits

Proverbs 5:3-5 (NASB)
*"For the lips of an adulteress drip honey and
smoother than oil is her speech;
but in the end, she is bitter as wormwood, sharp as a two-edged sword.
Her feet go down to death, her steps lay hold of Sheol."*

The single most powerful way an adulteress seduces her prey, besides the clothes that she wears and the way that she moves, are the words of her mouth. The seducing spirit draws the victim near through words as smooth as butter. The scriptures speak of this especially regarding men. Perhaps a man hasn't been noticed or appreciated for a long time. Perhaps he hasn't felt attractive or respected for a long time. If a man has been neglected sexually by his wife, the enticing words of a seducing woman working flattery will indeed minister to him. Let a man be warned to beware of flattery through any woman. Let a man of God heed the wisdom from God in these matters. Flirting and flattery make a deadly dangerous duo.

Proverbs 7:4-5 (NKJV)
*"Say to wisdom, 'You are my sister,' and call
understanding your nearest kin,
that they may keep you from the immoral woman, from
the seductress who flatters with her words."*

Proverbs 7:21-23 (NKJV)
*"With her enticing speech she caused him to yield,
with her flattering lips she seduced him.
Immediately he went after her, as an ox goes to the slaughter,
or as a fool to the correction of the stocks, till an arrow struck his liver.
As a bird hastens to the snare, he did not know it would cost his life."*

Flattery and the Antichrist

It is important to note that the tool of flattery is so powerful that it shall be one of the main ways the antichrist will come into power. Smooth words and cunning shall be his manner. He shall be one who is, incredibly skilled in his ability to flatter. You see, it is very hard to accuse a flatterer. He is saying all the right things in all the right ways. On the surface he is indicating charm and an agreeable spirit, but underneath all of this resides a monster.

> *Daniel 11:21 (Amplified)*
> *"... But he shall come in without warning in time of security and shall obtain the kingdom by flatteries, intrigues, and cunning hypocritical conduct."*

> *Daniel 11:32 (Amplified)*
> *"And such as violate the covenant he shall pervert and seduce with flatteries, but the people who know their God shall prove themselves strong and shall stand firm and do exploits (for God)."*

It is, as the Word of God says, the man who flatters has other things in mind, and they are not to support, edify or help you. In fact, we can count on the flatterer working his or her own agenda to move us out of the way so they can have the advantage. And this is what the antichrist will do; he will seek to move old systems out of the way to set up new systems of his own devices which shall ultimately lead to the bondage and destruction of all who seek to follow after God.

Flattery is an Issue of the Heart

Regardless of how flattery is used and who it comes through (including ourselves), it is never sanctioned or approved by God. It is not part of wisdom that comes from God. It is instead a part of that which is called false wisdom. We need to be aware that we not resort to flattery to gain an advantage or to obtain a desire. We also need to be aware of those who would approach us in a flattering way so as not to get caught in that trap and be deceived and taken advantage of. It is really all about the issues of our heart. How important it is to examine our motives and also to rightly discern the intentions of others. Let us then guard our hearts and heed Wisdom's call to be warned and admonished. In this way, we can be kept in Christ and our heart will be held in a sincere purity of motive and intention.

Proverbs 4:23-24 (NKJV)
"Keep your heart with all diligence, for out of it spring the issues of life. Put away from you a deceitful mouth, and put perverse lips far from you."

Chapter Thirteen

Wisdom to Protect from Deception

Beware of Deception

It is Jesus who emphatically and repeatedly said, "Take heed that no one deceives you" (Matthew 24:4). There will be a great onslaught of deception hitting the church in the last days. The Bible calls this the great falling away. This will be the ongoing warfare for the saints of God in the end times. There will be a last harvest for the devil - a great final sweep of humanity pouring into the jaws of hell. The master plan of the enemy is a well devised and a well targeted deception. Oh, how easily we can cast the thought aside and imagine that it would never be us that would be deceived. But the truth is: we are better armed when we think that it could actually happen to us, as author Jesse Penn Lewis states:

> *"The knowledge that it is possible to be deceived*
> *keeps the mind open to the truth*
> *and light from God, and is one of the primary conditions for the keeping*
> *power of God; whereas a closed mind to light*
> *and truth is a certain guarantee*
> *of deception by Satan at his earliest opportunity."*
>
> *- War on the Saints By Jesse Penn Lewis*

This is also reiterated in the following scripture:

I Corinthians 10:12 (NKJV)
"Therefore, let him who thinks he stands take heed lest he fall."

One of the best protections against deceit is to realize that we can indeed be deceived. Do not let an ounce of ignorance, pride, or defiance get in the way of this truth.

There are two kinds of deceivers. One deceiver is the type that does not know he is deceived. He presumes he is right, but he is woefully mistaken. Therefore, this type of deceiver is most convincing because he truly believes that he is okay and that he is on the right course. The other kind of deceiver is the one who knows quite well that he deceives. He has taken on the assignment from the devil and is led according to hell's agenda. He has no fear of God before his eyes. He forsook God a long time ago.

2 Timothy 3:13 (KJV)
"But evil men and seducers shall wax worse and worse, deceiving, and being deceived."

Notice the words "shall wax worse and worse," this indicates that there will be a certain momentum building up of deception on the face of the earth. The actual meaning suggests that deception will be accelerated at an alarming rate in the end times! Be very careful, Jesus said, for even His own most devoted servants will be targeted and led astray.

Mark 13:22 (American King James Version)
"For false Christs and false prophets will arise and show signs and wonders to deceive if possible, even the elect."

Seducing spirits working through people will do their best to turn you from God. People with seducing spirits can appear to be angels of light to those they seduce. So we must test the spirits for the scripture says, "Beloved, do not believe every spirit, but test the spirits, whether they are of God; because many false prophets have gone out into the world" (1 Jn. 4:1). And we must inspect the fruit of their lives for the scripture says, "By their fruits you will know them" (Matt. 7:20). These are the only ways to truly discern truth from error. Let no man deceive you. The Bible says there shall be a great falling away. A great one, not a small one. Let us not take God's words lightly. We must be lovers of truth. Thy Word is truth. We must be lovers of the Word of God.

The Holy Spirit Speaks to Us Regarding the Latter Days

1 Timothy 4:1 (NKJV)
"Now the Spirit expressly says that in
latter times some will depart from
the faith, giving heed to deceiving spirits and doctrines of demons."

Amplified Translation
"But the (Holy) Spirit distinctly and expressly declares that in latter times
some will turn away from the faith, giving
attention to deluding and seducing spirits
and doctrines that demons teach."

These spirits will be so good at seducing people that the person will not even realize they are encountering demonic activity. No one wants to take on a wrong spirit, so it has to be presented to us in a way which would be very appealing and convincing. There is no need to try to discern anything about exactly what kind of spirits will be causing all the problems with the people of God in the last days, as the Holy Spirit has already let us specifically know. The spirits at work are called deceiving, deluding, and seducing spirits. Further study reveals that these deceiving spirits from the Greek translation are called "Deamonion," which means spirit guides. We know that it is the job of the Holy Spirit to reveal and disclose things to the people of God and to guide them into all truth.

> *John 16:13 (NKJV)*
> *"However, when He, the Spirit of truth, has come, He will guide you into all truth; for He will not speak on His own authority, but whatever He hears He will speak; and He will tell you things to come."*

But spirit guides will work to be a counterfeit of the Holy Spirit in order to pull people off and guide them into all error. Therefore, it is imperative to know the Holy Spirit. The more we know the person of the Holy Spirit, the less able a false spirit will be able to draw us off. The Holy Spirit is fully aware that other spirits in the end times will seek to counterfeit Him and mimic Him and try to steal away the hearts of men and their allegiance to Christ. He sternly warns us of these coming events. Notice we will not be kept from the attempts of deceivers or deceiving spirits to seduce us. God has already warned us all about it in His Word; therefore, it is now our responsibility to beware and to be wise. This does not mean that the Holy Spirit won't warn us at times or reveal things to us at times that would cause us to avoid such dangers in this regard. But if we are not in tune with God, seeking Him frequently, or sensitive to His voice and promptings, we can easily be carried off into that which is not of God.

If we are "church hopping" with no church home and are not submitted to a pastor then we are setting ourselves up for a certain fall. Even still, one must be very aware of the doctrine they are sitting under Sunday after Sunday and who is laboring among them. Churches can change and fall away; some are even in danger of losing their lamp stand because they have lost the voice of God leading them, and the presence of God has departed. Churches can change. Paul bemoans the Corinthian church who is asleep at the wheel receiving that which is false. They were blithely unaware that they were putting up with deception in many forms by tolerating error through false things such as: another Jesus, a different spirit, (than the Holy Spirit) and a different gospel.

> *2 Corinthians 11:3-4 (NKJV)*
> *"But I fear, lest somehow, as the serpent deceived Eve by his craftiness, your minds may be corrupted from the simplicity that is in Christ. For if he who comes preaches another Jesus whom we have not preached, or if you receive a different spirit which you have not received, or a different gospel which you have not accepted – you may well put up with it!"*

Seduced by Seducing spirits

The thing about being seduced into wrong doctrine or led of a wrong spirit or a wrong voice is that the victim is not forced but goes willingly. The person does not even realize they are entering into deception and stepping out of their place of abiding in Christ. There is an accounting in the Book of Proverbs of the seducing ways of the strange woman. She is a picture of how seduction works. It is important to note that this word 'strange,' as in 'strange woman,' does not mean what we may think it means such as bizarre or weird, but instead means 'a stranger to the covenant.' She is considered a seductress, immoral, and adulterous.

> *Proverbs 2:16-19 (NASB)*
> *"To deliver you from the strange woman, from the adulteress who flatters with her words;*
> *that leaves the companion of her youth and forgets the covenant of her God;*
> *for her house sinks down to death and her tracks lead to the dead; none who go to her return again, nor do they reach the paths of life."*

The fact is, the same works of seduction that take place to seduce someone into being sexually immoral are the same ones that spiritually would seduce us into the arms of false doctrines and false spirits. False doctrines and spirits not only carry the assignment to seduce but also the power to seduce. The power comes from the kingdom of darkness. We see Paul speak of these seducing powers in terms of witchcraft.

> ***Galatians 3:1 (NKJV)***
> *"O foolish Galatians! Who has bewitched you*
> *that you should not obey the truth,*
> *before whose eyes Jesus Christ was clearly portrayed*
> *among you as crucified?"*
>
> ***Galatians 3:1 (Amplified)***
> *"...Who has fascinated or bewitched or cast a spell over you..."*

Note the Amplified Bible translation depicts a fuller description of the powers of seduction in increasing phases of demonic power, using the terms, to 'fascinate,' to 'bewitch' and 'to cast a spell over.' Let us take these three powers of seduction, and see what they really mean.

1. Seduction as in: To Fascinate

To fascinate literally means to "hold the attention of." It is not just getting the attention of - a car horn can do that. It's getting the attention and holding it there. Once the seducing spirit has adequately fascinated us and has our attention completely, it moves on to the next stage of deception - to secure its victim under its influence. It is important to note that deception works in stages. Indoctrination is a methodical well-planned process. Successive stages give way to a deeper and more demonic hold on the person.

2. Seduction as in: To Bewitch

The word bewitched or 'be-witched,' as in the working of witchcraft powers, to manipulate the soul. The *King James Version Dictionary* defines bewitched this way: "To gain control over through charm. To please to such a degree as to take away the power to resist. To bewitch also means to control by the art of pleasing." Can I say that there is a lot out there in the body of Christ today that preaches a flesh pleasing gospel and a world pleasing gospel versus a God-pleasing gospel? Many believe that we, the American church, are being steered off course quite a bit, and if we don't get back into balance with the truth of the Word and out from under our "bewitched" state, we may very well miss the mark. In any case, the Apostle Paul noticed that the church in Galatia had strayed and had gotten caught up in error through becoming 'bewitched.' Not even Paul could shake it off of them, though he tried repeatedly to shake some sense into them through his many wise questions. Finally in exasperation asking: "Have I therefore become your enemy because I tell you the truth?" (Gal. 4:16) They were seduced and wholly deceived, falling back under the law which placed them under a cursed state (Gal. 3:10, 5:4).

3. Seduction as in: To Cast a Spell On

To cast a spell on, is when the powers of darkness cause one to come under the complete influence of something or someone. The effect of a spell is an invisible binding of the mind. The mind becomes wholly submitted to a wrong spirit and sits in agreement with it. That agreement and submission to that wrong spirit gives demons the legal ground they need to bring about bondage. Have you ever heard of the word spellbound? Well, that is what it is: they are "bound" under a spell. The only thing that will break a spell is repenting and renouncing the lie and receiving and declaring the truth in its place.

Deception Happens in Stages

It is important to note that deception does not take place overnight; it happens slowly and to the unsuspecting. If we believe we are too spiritually mature to fall, we should beware.

Hebrews 2:1 (NKJV)
"Therefore, we must give the more earnest
heed to the things we have heard,
lest we drift away."

We always need to remain humble, accountable and open to correction concerning the wiles of deception. If we find we have been deceived, humility before God and man is the way to begin to be free. The process of deliverance also involves a revelation of the truth, deep repentance, healing and restoration in order for a person to get back to where they are abiding under Christ once more. Praise God that Jesus came to set the captives free.

A Prayer for those Needing Deliverance from False Ministry:

Lord Jesus, I repent and renounce any and all association or submission to false teachers, false doctrines, false prophets, and false spirits. I ask that you cleanse my spirit, soul, and body of any defilement associated with that which is false. I command, by the name of Jesus, that any cursed effects through these impartations and connections be made to leave me now in Jesus's name. I command any and all familiar spirits, counterfeit spirits, soothsayer spirits, spirit guides, spirits of error, and unclean spirits to go now and never return and to take all your ill effects with you out of my life forever. I now come out of agreement with all that is false and come into agreement with all that is true according to the Word of God. Lord, I ask that You break and sever all ties associated with any and all false leaders, false doctrines, false prophets and false prophecies, false ministries, and associations. Cleanse me from the defilements therein I pray. Close the door whereby these things entered, and hide me under the sheltering protection of Your wings. Redirect my life in truth and surround me with those who love the truth, walk in truth, and are led by truth. I ask You, Holy Spirit of the living God, to fill me afresh and anew and lead my life in the right way and along straight paths. It is in Jesus's name I pray. Amen.

Protection from Deception – A Prayer & Declaration: Proverbs 2

Father, I choose to receive Your words and treasure Your commandments within me. I incline my heart and ears to hear Your wisdom and choose to apply my heart to understanding. I cry out for discernment and lift up my voice for understanding, I seek her as silver, and search for her as for hidden treasures; so that I may understand the fear of the Lord, and find the knowledge of God.

I thank You Lord, that You give wisdom, and from Your mouth comes knowledge and understanding.

Thank You that You have wisdom stored up for me as I walk uprightly, and that You guard my paths in justice and preserve the way that I take. I pray that I may understand righteousness, justice, equity and every good path. I pray that Your wisdom would enter my heart and that Your knowledge would be pleasant to my soul, that discretion would preserve me and that understanding would keep me. Thank You that Your wisdom delivers me from the way of evil, and from the man who speaks perverse things. May Your wisdom deliver me from those who leave the paths of uprightness to walk in ways of darkness. May Your wisdom preserve me from those who rejoice in doing evil, and who delight in the perversity of wickedness. May Your wisdom protect me from those whose ways are crooked and who are devious in their paths. May Your wisdom deliver me from the strange woman, from those who seduce, from the spirit of Jezebel, the spirit of Delilah and all immoral people, and from those who flatter with their words. May your wisdom deliver me from those who forsake You and forget their covenant with You, and from those who take pathways toward death.

May I walk in the way of Your goodness and keep to the paths of righteousness that I may dwell in the land and remain in it as blameless. In Your mighty name I pray, Amen.

Chapter Fourteen

The Revelation and Wisdom of the Five Smooth Stones

I was in a difficult place in my life and was reflecting very deeply after a wrong choice I had made.

Places of pain teach us well. I was ardently seeking God for His wisdom to help me forge through the difficulty. His presence entered into this time in my life in such a significant way that it is hard to put into words. But, while I was studying the Word that day, the Lord gave me a significant revelation, and He called it: The Five Smooth Stones. He handed these stones individually to me and said,

"Hold these stones because these stones will keep you through any storm in this life, and they will help you with all your choices and decisions so that you may do well."

Isn't it wonderful that we have a God that wants us to do well! No matter what mistakes we may make or what wrong turns we may take, He is always a friend to the lonely, the hurting, the disillusioned, and those in crisis. So, it is at this time that I would like to share these stones with you. It is my great hope and intention that these five smooth stones enrich your life and your walk with Christ as it did mine. And so now I will take you into the Word of God where I was that day....

> *1 Samuel 17:38-39 (NKJV)*
> *"So Saul clothed David with his armor, and*
> *he put a bronze helmet on his head;*
> *he also clothed him with a coat of mail. David fastened*
> *his sword to his armor and tried to walk,*
> *for he had not tested them. And David said to Saul,*
> *'I cannot walk with these, for I have not tested*
> *them.' So David took them off."*

When you develop an anointing, the worst thing you can do is to let another clothe you. The battle seems formidable and impossible, and everyone else's garb seems so impressive, shiny, and strong. And here you are with nothing but a sling in hand. Somehow, now that it's time for the mother of all battles, you become convinced that you need something else or something more. It takes faith to trust in what God has given us and what God has developed in us, and to be wise as David was and walk out there with sling in hand. That's right, just you and that dinky old sling. So, there was Saul offering David his armor - how impressive and how generous of him! Sometimes I think this is where David won the battle, right there with Saul, before he even hit the field with Goliath looming over him. It was there, behind the scenes, one warrior to another, conversing and debating strategy to meet the foe. You see, battles are not necessarily fought and won out on the field; they are fought and wrestled out behind the scenes, in the back rooms of preparation. You see God had already prepared David, just as God has prepared us who seek Him out for wisdom. And if we are not careful, we will let go of our faith, minimize the anointing, and take the offer the fleshly man is so eager to provide. But David refused Saul's offer of his armor, saying, "I cannot walk in these" (1 Samuel 17:39). And so it is true, we cannot walk in another man's armor as God has given us our own. This moment was a test of David's faith, to simply trust in the anointing that God had given him.

And David Took His Staff in Hand

1 Samuel 17:40 (NKJV)
*"Then he took his staff in his hand; and chose for himself five smooth stones
from the brook, and put them in a shepherd's
bag, in a pouch which he had,
and his sling was in his hand. And he drew near to the Philistine."*

The Staff: Our Authority in Christ

David took his staff in his hand. The staff is representative of one's authority in Christ. It is the staff that goes before and holds one up. It is the staff that is the head, and the head is Christ. We do not take hold of who we are in ourselves; we take hold of who we are in Christ. Jesus has given us all manner of authority as the scripture so clearly says:

Luke 10:19 (NKJV)
*"Behold, I give you the authority to trample on serpents
and scorpions, and over all the power of the enemy,
and nothing shall by any means hurt you."*

Gathering Stones

Although Christ has given us this authority, we have to pick it up. We need to take hold of the staff we have been given by Christ and walk with it. It does not carry itself. We must take it with us and walk in the authority of Christ. So David takes his staff in hand and chooses five smooth stones from the brook. He finds the stones in the brook, in the stream of God's Word so to speak. He did not choose stones off of the earth but out of the water. It is said in scripture that we are washed by the "water through the Word." (Ephesians 5:26) We know what happens to us as Christians when we fail to cleanse ourselves in the Word daily. The things of the earth begin to cling to us. David finds what he needs for battle searching through the pure reflective waters of the Word of God. He then puts the stones he finds there in his shepherd's bag. The pouch, we can say, is symbolic of his heart. Is it not true that the Psalmist David has said… "Thy words have I hidden in my heart that I may not sin against Thee" (Psalm 119:11). As we read the Word, we see and notice certain scriptures that we need for our lives, so we pick up that stone from the stream. We may further read and notice a scripture that is one the Holy Spirit wants us to use, so we pick up that one too; gathering stones and placing them to memory, and then into the heart where they are kept safe to be stored and used at the proper time.

Our Authority in Christ and the Anointing

David has prepared himself taking up his staff in one hand which is symbolic of the authority he has in Christ. He has located the stones (the scriptures he would need for battle) and placed them in the pouch of his heart. He then takes his sling in the other hand and approaches the Philistine. The sling is representative of the anointing. The sling is the skillful work that God had developed in David's life. At first glance it doesn't look like much - just a dirty old sling, but the worn appearance of it shows that it had been used many times. It is said that a stone thrown skillfully by a warrior could travel upwards of one hundred miles per hour. It is even said of some warriors that their accuracy was so perfect that they could split hairs. With the authority of Christ in one hand (the staff), and the sling in the other hand (the anointing), David approached the Philistine.

We see here the key elements to gaining the victory in our lives:

1. **Our Authority in Christ:** We have to take it up and use it
2. **The Word of God:** Hidden in our heart
3. **The Anointing:** The gift of God that has been developed in our life that we have been faithful and obedient to exercise.

With these three key elements in place, David approached the Philistine. It is interesting to know that Philistine means, "to wallow in the dust." His name reveals his destiny. The giant is brought down to wallow in the dust of defeat. I don't know what the giant is in your life or what he is saying to you, but we are given three key principles of warfare to bring it down. Many Christians go through battles with nothing but a pleading prayer to be delivered. This is not a bad thing but there is more, so much more. David did not sit around and wait for God to handle this giant. He took on the battle, squared off before the enemy, and worked what God had given him and what God had developed in him. Can God do any less with us? I don't think so. Let us go now and gather some stones. I will show you the ones that the Lord gave to me out of the brook of His Word. It was as if He said,

"Here, take these. These are the ones that are the keys to any battle you will ever face. They will always work. They have been tried and they are true. And with these stones you will never encounter that kind of defeat again."

THE FIRST SMOOTH STONE

The Stone of Humility

Humility is the foundation of all virtues and the most precious and necessary of all the stones. Humility is a choice and the intentional act of a person to make their self lower; to bow and to yield and to willingly submit. This does not come naturally to the flesh. The flesh part of ourselves wants to be seen, heard, known, and recognized. But true humility is happy in the back seat, being the last in line, and going unnoticed and barely heard. A person with the character of humility does not insist on their own way. Humility does not contend, and it does not judge nor take offense.

Humility is a Covering

In the spirit realm, humility is recognized as a covering. Without it we are seen as naked and exposed. Yet with the cloak of humility, we are recognized as protected and covered by God. One cannot see flesh in humility but with pride, one's flesh is hanging out all over the place. This is why the scripture says for us to actually clothe ourselves with humility.

1 Peter 5:5 (NIV)
"...All of you, clothe yourselves with humility toward one another, because, 'God opposes the proud and gives grace to the humble.'"

It's like getting dressed. We are to literally put humility on ourselves. As a Christian, when we open the closet door to choose our clothes for the day, one of the things we always need to put on is the cloak of humility. This is the servant's attire. Are you a servant of God? Then let's cull through the racks of our closet and locate the garment of humility and put it on each day. This is the mark of Christ Himself. This is to His glory.

1 Peter 5:5-6 (Amplified)
"Likewise, you who are younger and of lesser rank, be subject to the elders (the ministers and spiritual guides of the church) - [giving them due respect and yielding to their counsel]. Clothe (apron) yourselves, all of you, with humility [as the garb of a servant, so that its covering cannot possibly be stripped from you, with freedom from pride and arrogance] toward one another. For God sets Himself against the proud (the insolent, the overbearing, the disdainful, the presumptuous, the boastful) - [and He opposes, frustrates, and defeats them], but gives grace (favor, blessing) to the humble. Therefore, humble yourselves [demote, lower yourselves in your own estimation] under the mighty hand of God, that in due time He may exalt you ..."

The Illusive Nature of Pride

The astonishing thing about pride is that we often do not recognize it in ourselves. The fact is, we can be too proud to see see our own pride. Pride is very illusive. Only in humility is the veil lifted. Therefore, we must ask the Lord to show us where pride is lurking in our lives. You do not have to wonder if it's there. We all have it as part of our flesh nature, unfortunately. Pride tends to rear its ugly head without us even knowing it through things like offense, contention, thinking more highly of ourselves than we ought, judging others, taking on airs of superiority, just to name a few. It has been said that, "Pride is like bad breath, everyone knows you have it but you!" We desperately need some kind soul to let us know so that we can see ourselves and repent! The Holy Spirit, our trusted Counselor, will let us know if we are sensitive to His voice and promptings. If not, we shall soon be exposed and embarrassed. Nothing like a dose of humiliation to bring about the needed humility we need in our lives. I have come up with my own analogy for pride, and it is this: Pride is like a hospital gown, you walk through the corridors of life and think you are just fine, but everyone in the hallway sees your flap is open, and your backside is in full view for all to see!

Humility Attracts God

Humility is something that attracts God to us, and pride is something that distances God from us. We need to understand these things so that we can have the nearness of God in our lives always.

Psalm 138:6 (BSB)
*"Though the Lord is on high, He attends to the
lowly, but the proud He knows from afar."*

Psalm 138:6 (Amplified Version)
*"For though the Lord is high, yet has He respect to the
lowly [bringing them into fellowship with Him];
but the proud and haughty He knows and recognizes [only] at a distance."*

Humility and Brokenness

Do you feel that God is far away? Then, perhaps, as we humble ourselves under His hand and become contrite and even broken, we will sense His presence begin to stir. Have you ever done that? Have you ever placed yourself under God and just yielded in the difficult circumstance and felt the breaking? Have you ever gone up to the altar and met that person there who would pray for you and felt the breaking and things all fall apart? This is humility at work. It's the power of brokenness. God loves this because our hard exterior has cracked and He can come in. Sometimes God can do His deepest and best work when the jar of self breaks. When self becomes broken before God, it is a great thing. In fact, this is where greatness begins.

Isaiah 57:15 (NIV)
"... I live in a high and holy place, but also with him who is contrite and lowly in spirit, to revive the spirit of the lowly and to revive the heart of the contrite."

Humility is a Battle Stone

This is an odd thing. Humility and war do not seem to go together at all. In fact, the last thing I would want to fight a battle with as a weapon is humility. But, it was the stone of humility that Christ used to overcome and bring the victory for us all. This is why the devil was so beaten in the end - he didn't see it coming. The challenge to fight, to get provoked, and to strike back was continually put before Jesus. The temptation to say something in His own defense or to call upon the legions of angels that would have arrived instantaneously on the scene, to call down wrath, or to get off the rugged cross was all a viable possibility, but He was using the humility stone. It was the perfect stone for this battle because it disguised itself as losing when in fact it was winning. That's the beauty and luster of this stone. To the flesh, you are going down for the count, but in the spirit, you are being elevated. Will we ever understand the ways of God? But, here is Jesus winning the battle against Satan and his foul hordes of cruel demons with the simple single lone stone of humility, hitting the devil right in the middle of his forehead. He's going down, folks, and he indeed has fallen!

> *Philippians 2:8-11 (NKJV)*
> *"And being found in appearance as a man, He humbled Himself and became obedient to the point of death, even the death of the cross. Therefore, God also has highly exalted Him and given Him the name which is above every name, that at the name of Jesus every knee should bow, of those in heaven, and of those on earth, and of those under the earth, and that every tongue should confess that Jesus Christ is Lord, to the glory of God the Father."*

THE SECOND SMOOTH STONE

The Stone of Grace

Grace has a two-fold definition. Grace is the undeserved and unmerited favor of God, and grace is also God's strength and ability infused into the believer in order to accomplish and achieve a purpose. How do we acquire this stone of grace? Well, the scripture says it comes only by way of humility. This means that you must have the first stone of humility working in your life before you can receive the grace stone. The secret of the five smooth stones is not just the stones in and of themselves, but it is their vital connection to one another as well. Grace is something God gives, but it is only to the humble. Let's see this in scripture:

> *James 4:6 (ESV)*
> *"... God opposes the proud but gives grace to the humble."*

Paul Receives the Stone of Grace

Paul had an ongoing battle with something he called, "a thorn in his flesh." It has now become a term that we use for something that is painful and aggravating on a continual basis. The only way to alleviate the pain would be to have the thorn removed. This is logical, isn't it? But not to God. God's remedy for this affliction was not removal but to give Paul a stone for the pouch of his heart called grace. I can hear Paul now, can't you?

"But God, this is not going to do anything! You are supposed to be my deliverer!"

And it is then that the Lord speaks and thus says,

> "My grace is sufficient for thee because My strength is made perfect in weakness."

Here it is in the scripture:

> *2 Corinthians 12:8-9 (NKJV)*
> *"Concerning this thing I pleaded with the Lord*
> *three times that it might depart from me.*
> *And He said to me, 'My grace is sufficient for you, for*
> *My strength is made perfect in weakness ...'"*

He pleaded three times. He kept going back saying, in essence,

> "This stone isn't going to work in this battle - I need to be radically delivered!"

Isn't this also the way we are when we realize, in a difficult circumstance or hardship, that God is *not* going to wave the magic wand and get us out of our difficulty? Instead, He is going to work very mightily, but it will be as we are infused with His ability and strength to endure and overcome and be victorious through it. So many times, we are not delivered out of it but through it. We do come out the other side. And we say, looking back,

> "How in the world did I ever make it through? How did I endure such difficulty?" ·

And then we reflect and know... it was the grace stone. God somehow caused me to be able to go through this difficulty against all odds. I am indeed victorious through Christ who strengthens me!

> *Philippians 4: 13 (Amplified)*
> *"I have strength for all things in Christ Who empowers me [I am ready for anything and equal to anything through Him Who infuses inner strength into me; I am self-sufficient in Christ's sufficiency]."*

Just You and the Grace of God

Are you fighting a battle and wondering why God isn't "delivering" you? Perhaps, He has grace for you but you haven't found it yet. I know it is not the stone you may want for the battle, but it will cause you to overcome. This is the secret that you need to know: God wants to fight the battle with you as a participant with Him and not as an onlooker. He wants to get into the field of battle with you to cause you to overcome. You are not in Kindergarten anymore. God is taking you higher. David met the Philistine with a grace stone in his pouch. Paul continued on with the thorn in his flesh by grace as well. Gideon faced the Midianites with a grace stone at work inside of him fighting all manner of fear. They all were in that place with God, where God doesn't take you out of the battle, nor does He win it for you. Instead, He entreats you to win the battle by His grace alone. So many Christians sit on the bleachers waiting for God to win them the battle. We have these lofty ideas about how we think God should help us with our battles. Not so fast. We've jumped the starter's mark. We need to have the referee reset the timer and begin again, and this time run the race according to heaven's agenda.

Come to the Throne of Grace

We are called to come to the throne of grace, to find our much needed help in our time of need. He is waiting for us to come. He wants to endow us so that will see that His power is made perfect in our weakness.

(2 Cor. 12:9) Grace is always available to the believer. Have you a need, a hardship, a heart wrenching situation, or an unending saga of troubles that never seem to end? Then you are in sore need of the faithful stone of grace. And the only place to get that stone is the throne of grace.

> ***Hebrews 4:16 (Amplified)***
> *"Let us then fearlessly and confidently and boldly draw near to the throne of grace (the throne of God's unmerited favor to us sinners), that we may receive mercy [for our failures] and find grace to help in good time for every need [appropriate help and well-timed help, coming just when we need it]."*

THE THIRD SMOOTH STONE

The Stone of Wisdom

The stone of wisdom comes only with the first stone of humility also. Unless we have the stone of humility working in our lives, we cannot receive wisdom. Here is the scripture confirming this:

> ***Proverbs 11: 2 (NIV)***
> *"When pride comes, then comes disgrace, but with humility comes wisdom."*

Humility and godly wisdom go together. You cannot have one without the other. We see it again expressed in the book of James:

> ***James 3:13 (NIV)***
> *"Who is wise and understanding among you?*
> *Let him show it by their good life,*
> *by deeds done in the humility that comes from wisdom."*

They go together. One who is humble is probably wise. One who is wise is probably humble. The opposites go together as well. One who is proud is certainly foolish. One who is foolish is, in fact, proud. The only way to receive godly wisdom is to do what the scripture says: Ask for it. This may seem elementary, but we don't ask much of the time. We assume we are already there. But the humble will most certainly ask. They understand already that they know little or nothing, compared to God who knows everything.

> ### *James 1:5 (NIV)*
> *"If any of you lacks wisdom, he should ask God, who gives generously to all without finding fault, and it will be given to you."*

James was writing this in terms of a battle. The previous text states that the believer encounters trials and sufferings often, and so James exhorts the believer to get the stone of wisdom to fight with, through the time of difficulty. Get God's mind on the matter. Wisdom is there for the asking - His insight - His counsel - His instruction - His discernment - His strategy - His knowledge - His course of action - His plan - His viewpoint - His opinion - His secrets - His guidance .... yes, all these and more are all facets of wisdom from God that are available to the believer who asks. Wisdom is a many faceted diamond with different reflections from every viewpoint imaginable.

God has Wisdom Stored up for Us

Stored up for us in heaven is the wisdom we need for the battles we fight. God dispenses the wisdom as needed when asked. Have you placed an order lately? Are you on the front lines of some battlefield in your life in which you need to know where all the flack is coming from, and what would be the best way to handle it? Are you in the trenches of a situation needing to radio in somewhere for supplies and assistance? Then, call into heaven's quarters and put a demand on the supply up there. Get the wisdom. Fight with heaven's support.

> ### *Proverbs 2:6 -7 (NASB)*
> *"For the Lord gives wisdom; from His mouth come knowledge and understanding.*
> *He stores up sound wisdom for the upright ..."*

The Wisdom called Divine Strategy

We need, definitely need, divine strategy to fight our battles. God has that. Just read about the battles fought by Israel, and notice how each victory occurred through some divine strategy of God. It stands to reason then that if God had divine strategy for natural Israel that He also has divine strategy for spiritual Israel - that would be us.

Proverbs 20:18 (NKJV)
"Plans are established by counsel; by wise counsel wage war."

Know Your Strengths and Weaknesses

In our walk with God, we know that we fight the war many times of temptation - the temptation to sin. Temptation to step a step beyond. Temptation to do it our way. Temptation to take another course than the one God has prescribed. There are a thousand and one temptations the believer is confronted with in this life. One of the best ways to fight temptation is to recognize your weakness for what it is and to plan a strategy of resistance so that when it comes on around to present itself to you, (and it most assuredly will), you already have a plan, a strategy in place to combat it and take it down. Many people succumb over and over again but never sit down - pen in hand - and lay out the plan - a personal plan for resistance and victory. What is your wisdom? What is your strategy for the war that seeks to level you? God knows our adversary has scoped you out enough and consulted with his evil minions enough to plan to bring a wicked scheme to pass at just the right time, in just the right place, to take you out - again. So what is your strategy for your next round with the enemy? What is your plan? Does it have a sense of heavenly counsel about it?

A good athlete will study his opponent's strengths and weaknesses. They will view videos of the games the opponent has previously played, study them closely, and will look to see where that athlete is weak or infirmed. Then he or she will plan accordingly. He or she will then play the game focusing most of his or her attention on the opponent's weaknesses, continually looking for an opening to take the best shot. And so now, what makes you think that the most formidable enemy we have in this life is not doing the same thing? He most certainly is. You can read the accounting of Job and see how Satan was trying to gain viewpoints of Job to get in and take him down. You can see the strategy of Satan at work against David when David took the census of Israel. You can sense the strategy of Satan at work when Peter was approached with probing questions at the time of Christ's trial and crucifixion. Not only is the plan of Satan worked out, the timing is impeccable as well. So, I entreat you, what is your strategy to overcome the adversary in your situation? Do you even have one? The usual common place thinking about this is,

"Well, I'll handle it when it comes …. It'll work out."

Many a strong man has been led away easily and met with shipwrecking their faith, through lack of preparedness or neglecting to think through issues of one's own weaknesses and vulnerabilities. Strong good men - strong good ministries - strong good people. And so now we must ask ourselves, what makes us think we are stronger or better than them? Don't be like Samson with your sin or weak inclination, going back for more, thinking that your special uniqueness in Christ will protect you from the evil one. It's time to wake up, wise up, and get the redemptive wisdom of God for your life. Develop your personal strategy whereby you would overcome. You know victory is taken by force. The righteous take it by force. That means on purpose.

Matthew 11:12 (NKJV)
"And from the days of John the Baptist until now the kingdom of heaven suffers violence, and the violent take it by force."

In all our Getting, Let's Get Wisdom

Proverbs 4: 5-7 (NKJV)
"Get wisdom! Get understanding! Do not forget, nor turn away from the words of my mouth. Do not forsake her, and she will preserve you; love her, and she will keep you. Wisdom is the principal thing; therefore, get wisdom. And in all your getting, get understanding."

Notice the exclamation points in the first line of the scripture above. What does this mean? It is an emphasis. It is a raised voice lifting itself up out of the page more strongly than the other words. It means that heaven is shouting to us from the grand stands - the great cloud of witnesses cheers us on to get wisdom and to get understanding, "Get it! Get it! Get it!"

THE FOURTH SMOOTH STONE

The Stone of Worship

True worship causes God to draw near. If our worship fails to draw the Lord near then we have not worshiped. Self is still in the way. What does worship mean? It means to bow low. Again, we see in this fourth stone that the sense of a certain humility is involved. Worship also means to pay homage to. Homage is not a word that we use much these days. Homage is an expression of high regard and deep respect. It attests to the worth of something and pays tribute or homage and is many times done on bended knee. To lower oneself further would be to lay prostrate. It is a certain abandoned surrender made by the naked humble self before his or her acknowledged Creator. Creature to Creator communion and the awesome awareness of such a thing. Many times this attitude of worship will acknowledge oneself as a vessel surrendered to the Lord, made wholly available to be used in whatever way the Lord Himself would please.

Worship Which Draws the Lord Near

Psalm 22:3 (NKJV)
"But You are holy, enthroned in the praises of Israel."

It is His presence that we all desire. It is through the means of praise and worship that we can make an entrance way for our King to pass by us. This scripture says that Jesus is literally carried in through the praises of His people, that in fact, He is "enthroned" through the praise. He literally rides in as we praise Him. What a picture!

His Presence Brings His Power

One would not think of worship as a stone for battle, but it indeed can be. Why is this so? It is so because with His presence comes also His power. The three successive and progressive phases are these: Praise - Presence - Power. The three P's, if you will. It is a formula or strategy for certain battles, and we have our examples from the Old Testament. The fact of the matter is that there are some battles that are only going to be won and overcome through the power of praise. It may be the last thing that you feel like doing at times, but it is the very thing that will knock the enemy out and down for the count. The devil does not want you to get a hold of this concept but in one of the fiercest battles in the Old Testament, we see that this particular stone was, in fact, the victory.

Praising in the Midst of Battle

2 Chronicles 20:21-22 (NKJV)
"And when he had consulted with the people, he appointed those who should sing to the Lord, and who should praise the beauty of holiness, as they went out before the army and were saying: 'Praise the Lord, for His mercy endures forever.' Now when they began to sing and to praise, the Lord set ambushes against the people of Ammon, Moab, and Mount Seir, who had come against Judah; and they were defeated."

Praise invokes God's presence to rule. God's presence, ushered in through the praise, confounded these three formidable armies. Some scholars actually say that the ambush involved angelic action. Also related was that dissension and feuds broke out in the enemy ranks. In any case, the connection between praise to God and the defeat of the enemy is clear.

Are you facing a battle at this time? Are there forces pressing hard against your life or the life of your family? Then consider the worship stone. It could be the one for the battle you are encountering. It may seem absurd, but we are considering a heavenly principle and not an earthly one. I will tell you right now that there are some battles that we fight that can only be fought and won by praising our way through it. It can be a short battle or one in which we are called upon to prevail in for a season. However, if you sense the Lord's presence as you praise, if you sense a lifting of the burden, if you feel a breaking of the power from that praise that you are engaged in, then that may be the stone to use. Once His presence comes in, He will take it from there, and you will have a better sense of what is going on and how to proceed.

Worship Became the Place for Healing

I heard this story of a woman about ten years ago who had been diagnosed with breast cancer. She was standing for her healing. She noticed that in her seeking the Lord through prayer, fasting, and praise, when she worshiped the Lord, she would feel better. It was as if she had stepped into a zone or realm of some kind. It is not that prayer was bad or fasting was not great, but she couldn't help but notice that when she spent time with God in worship, she was ushered into a whole new sense of her authority as a believer, and she really felt as if she was progressing past the disease. Being a devoted Christian, she attended church faithfully as well as other meetings and prayer groups. She wanted to receive everything she needed to come into complete healing. One prayer meeting that she went to taught on powerful warfare techniques that would guarantee victory against all kinds of battles. So, being eager to overcome her life-threatening situation, she took on this new level of warfare for her program for healing. Soon, she was heavily engaged, but over time she noticed she began to get worse instead of better. She decided to get some counsel on the matter from a very wise Christian. The Christian asked her this question:

> "Where is the place of His presence? When you devote yourself in your many activities, where have you sensed His presence the most clearly, the most sweetly, the most strongly?"

She thought a moment and reflected and said,

> "Well actually, a few months back I was simply making time to worship Him in my own way, in the midst of this trial and I noticed that there was always a lifting of the burden and always a strong sense of His presence and power in my midst."

"Well then," said the counselor, "Why is it that you have stopped?"

And she said,

> "I stopped because I thought I needed something more powerful, and I was so impressed by the spiritual warfare principles that I was taught that I thought I would apply them to this situation."

The counselor looked intently into her eyes and said,

> "If the place of His presence was in worship, then go back to the place where you found Him."

It is not that the warfare principles were bad or in error, but for her it was not the right battle stone for the occasion in her life. The anointing for victory for her particular battle was found in the place of praise and worship. This tells us that we must not be drawn off and distracted by what initially sounds so impressive and lofty, but instead, we need to listen and recognize that the Lord, through His powerful Holy Spirit, has already revealed to us what the victory plan is for our crisis situation. If He has not revealed these things to us yet, then we can keep seeking Him and testing the places where His presence for victory may be sensed. God may seem to be hiding, but it is more likely that He wants us to discover Him and to locate the powerful anointing needed and reserved for our victory.

Oh yes, in case you are wondering, the woman was healed! In her dire battle it was the worship stone which brought the victory. Like Jehoshophat, she found that heaven took on the battle as she stood in her place of praise and worship, and soon the cursed assignment sent to destroy her life became null and void.

THE FIFTH SMOOTH STONE

The Stone called: The Fellowship of His Sufferings

The fifth and final stone the Lord gave to me was the stone called *The Fellowship of His Sufferings*. At first I was not quite sure this is what

He said, but He reiterated to me that this was the last smooth stone and He gave it to me to put into the pouch of my heart. I knew that this stone was all about the cross and that it was very costly. And soon I found the scripture:

Philippians 3:10-11 (NKJV)
"... that I may know Him and the power of His resurrection, and the fellowship of His sufferings, being conformed to His death, if, by any means, I may attain to the resurrection from the dead."

The Cross

I had a person tell me once that she had tried everything to overcome this ongoing negative circumstance in her life. She had prayed, fasted, stood on the Word, worshiped, and I am sure, had done a host of other things to try to alleviate the ongoing pain and hardship of her difficult situation. She was making the final frustrating assessment that nothing worked for her. It was then that I knew she was called to use this costly stone called *The Fellowship of His Sufferings* for her battle. It is not a stone that one wants to use because it costs you everything, and you have to die to your will, but it is the most precious of all stones to use because it yields the greatest reward. So, I said to her, "If your situation is not being lessened or alleviated in any way by all these means that you have tried, then it is because it is a cross."

She looked up at me quizzically,

"What?"

And I said to her gently,

"It's not going away because it is a cross. You are being invited by Christ to share in the fellowship of His sufferings - to become identified with Him in this place of your trial. Stop fighting the process and allow Him to take you through the cross and into the resurrection. You won't come out the same, and you will know Christ more intimately than you have ever known Him before."

I didn't speak these words without some knowledge, as years before I encountered the same kind of thing and it seemed I had no one to help me. I soon spoke to an older woman in our church about it who had been through a lot in her life. She was also the 'house prophet' at that church. She told me quite emphatically that what I was going through was a cross. That through the trial of it God was accomplishing something greater. Then she said, "Don't worry honey, the first cross is the worst because you fight against it and do not understand what is going on. But as you continue your walk with the Lord, you will recognize when a situation or a problem is actually a cross for you to die on. You will also soon understand that it is just better to die to that thing than to try to fight it. Just let God have His way and yield to Him and He will bring you through to the other side."

And so I was finally briefed on the reality of my battle. It was not what I wanted to hear, but it sure helped me see my battle in a way I had never seen it before. And I entered into the fellowship of His sufferings and came to know Christ in a way I had never known Him before. What is it about pain and suffering, whereby His presence becomes so real and tangible to us? I don't know exactly but it's all part of the wondrous mystery of the cross.

Keys to Enduring the Cross

The final smooth stone called *The Fellowship of His Sufferings* contains in it the ability to endure the cross. Many times we fight the cross. We avoid the cross. We work an agenda to get off of the cross. But the call is to die. It's not to win. It is to lose. It's not to gain but to suffer the utter defeat of it all. It's not to be covered up, but it is to be stripped down. It's not to defend one's self, but it's to allow the charges to stick. It's not to proclaim one's innocence, but to be found guilty though innocent. Make no mistake this stone is not cheap!

The secret or revelation the Lord gave me of *The Fellowship of His Sufferings Stone* is found in cultivating all the other previous stones in your life. You will need the other stones to allow the cross to do its work in you.

1. It will take Humility *The Humility Stone*, to allow the humiliation of the cross to work in your life. "He humbled Himself and became obedient to death - even death on a cross ..." (Philippians 2:8).

2. It will take Grace *The Grace Stone*, to endure the cross, which is the fellowship of His sufferings. His grace is His ability and strength infused into us.

3. It will take Wisdom *The Wisdom Stone*, to understand this powerful work of God in our lives - the cross will no longer be a mystery but we will understand. "For the message of the cross is foolishness to those who are perishing, but to us who are being saved, it is the power of God" (1 Corinthians 1:18).

4. It will take Worship *The Worship Stone*, a complete sacrificial love and adoration to do this for Christ. " ... indeed we share in His sufferings in order that we may also share in His glory..." (Romans 8:17).

In essence, humility, grace, wisdom and worship will help us in and through the fellowship of His sufferings. And in that sacred place we will have His sweet presence and fellowship.

Do you have a battle you can no longer fight? Have you become weary with the unending strain? Then release yourself fully to the work of the cross and die. Enter into the fellowship of His sufferings and you will find true life. For as you choose to lose your life, the scriptures say that, you indeed will find it. "For whoever wants to save his life will lose it, but whoever loses his life for My sake will find it." (Mt. 16:24) If you resist and hold on to your life, you will miss the higher life He wants you to have. And you will miss the greater work He desires to do in you to conform you to His image.

Romans 8:18 (NKJV)
"For I consider that the sufferings of this present time are not worthy to be compared with the glory which shall be revealed in us."

And so is the wisdom and revelation of the five smooth stones.

Chapter Fifteen

The Revelation and Wisdom of the Fear of the Lord

Exodus 20:20 (NKJV)
"... Do not fear; for God has come to test you,
and that His fear may be before you, so that you may not sin."

The following is an encounter I had with Father God in the very early days of my walk as a Christian. It was through divine providence that I had pastors at the time who helped me handle this experience. I cannot stress enough how important it is to have pastors that really know God, have years of experience walking the walk, and have come to know His presence, His holiness, and His ways. I came trembling to them in a state of complete disorientation after this encounter. If I had not had pastors that were older and well-versed in the Word and with God, I am not sure how I would have assembled the experience in my mind by myself. They knew I had encountered God. After I pulled myself together and related everything, they strongly encouraged me to share this experience at the midweek service. I hesitated, but they exhorted that the church needed to hear, and so I did. Afterwards, in the back of the room was a man named Dennis. He was an ex-Hell's Angel's biker who had been gloriously saved and delivered by God. Anyway, he raised his hand and was so persistent. The pastor asked him to share and he said, "I know what she is talking about. I had a shocking wave of fear come over me when I was just home from work last week as I was changing into my casual clothes." Then Dennis asked me what day and time it was that it happened so I told him, and he said it was the exact same day and time that the fear of God hit him. He said the fear threw him to the floor to pay homage to the Almighty. Then he said he heard the words, "Call Karen and comfort her in her time of distress… Call Karen…" and he continued and said, "I am so sorry I did not call you to be a comfort to you and to be a witness to you that God was in your midst. Please forgive me!" Then the pastor admonished him a little because I was so traumatized when I came to see them. They had to spend significant time comforting and assuring me of God's love and that I was not going to go to hell. I had also thought the whole church had seen me standing before God and they had to assure me that was not so. Here, without further prefacing is the accounting of what happened.

I was working long hours at a high-end design firm. The pressure was constant and the project deadlines made each day a nearly impossible feat. I had a boss who was demanding and as a young Christian, I did not take to her management style very well. Soon, I was ranting with all the other workers there, criticizing the decisions, and complaining about the tight schedules and demands. My mouth was beginning to get me in trouble with God. I could sense conviction and the grieving of the Holy Spirit as I went into my prayer times early in the morning.

For months I wrestled with this sin issue in my life, and then would find myself back in the tension-filled situation at work only to start up with the mouth again. It was a cycle of sin and confession, sin and confession, sin and confession. It was the sin that so easily entangles (Hebrews 12:1). I wanted God to change me, and He wanted me to change for Him. Does anyone know what I am talking about? I pressed into God and said, "Lord, I can't change this, please change me. Please cause me to stop." But I did not realize what I was asking. If I had known what I was about to experience I would have gladly just worked the necessary discipline in my life to get the sin out of my life. But I just kept pressing it with God for Him to do the work to change me.

Then one night as I was reading the Word, I was arrested by a scripture in the Book of James. I felt a weight to it as I read it. There was a heavy sternness about it which made me uneasy causing me to tremble. I did what I could to shake the deep sense of foreboding off me and went to sleep. Being so young in the Lord, I was completely unfamiliar with the reality of God's ability to chastise or bring discipline to a saint. This was the scripture that arrested me that night:

James 5:9 (NKJV)
"Do not grumble against one another, brethren, lest you be condemned. Behold, the Judge is standing at the door!"

The next day I went to work, and in the afternoon, I began to sense a strong discomfort. It was an awareness that something was wrong - very wrong. I could not shake it. For three days it steadily and slowly became more and more intense. I did not know this, but it was God Almighty steadily coming near. Soon, I could not focus or concentrate. I would drive home to see if anything was wrong there. Nothing would be wrong, so I would drive back to work and nothing was wrong there. But this awful prevailing sense of dread that something was very wrong was overwhelming me. I stopped eating on the second day. My complete attention was riveted on what could be wrong. It felt as if I had done something terrible, but I could not figure out what! It was like a freight train coming toward me, but I could not see it to get out of the way. Soon, I began to be panicky. The smallest unexpected sound or sudden movement shook me to the core. Finally, I left work in the afternoon of the third day to go home and just go to bed. I was changing out of my clothes and in the state of nakedness when an all-consuming fear of the Lord swallowed me up in a terror that simply cannot be put into words. I dove into my bed scrambling for cover. At the time, I did not know it was the fear of the Lord, but it did not take too long to figure out that God was in the midst and not in a good way! The next instant I was standing before God as one being judged. I was, as the scripture exactly says, "naked and ashamed." All I can tell you is that I was before the Judge of the whole universe. Then, I remembered the scripture that had arrested me a few nights before... "Behold the Judge is standing at the door!" And so there I stood naked before God Almighty with His holy angels behind me.

Hebrews 4:13 (NKJV)
*"And there is no creature hidden from His sight,
but all things are naked and open
to the eyes of Him to whom we must give account."*

Then came the inquiry from God. His questions to me were relentlessly pounding my being, wanting answers about my various contentions. As I would prepare to respond, the answer would come out of my mouth before I even had a chance to think about it! Just so you know, there will be no "editing" in heaven. The heart is laid open for all to see, know and hear. My heart was speaking the harsh reality of the truth before God. I became mad at my own heart. I began speaking to my heart saying,

> "Why did you say that! You idiot... I can't believe you condemned me!"

Yet, my own heart and all its contents did just that- it condemned me. (1 John 3:20-21)

As the inquiry continued, I became lesser and lesser and smaller and smaller, pressed down lower, and lower still until I loathed myself and became as an insignificant worm of slime on the face of the ground. And then the words came blasting from the Almighty saying,

> "Will the one who contends with the Almighty correct Him?" (Job 40:2) I said,

> "No, No. I shall not! Please God, forgive me. I know not what I say!"

I was now convinced I was going to hell and over on the right side, there was an altar that I was called to lay upon, and I knew I was going to die. I was sentenced and the verdict was just. I remember the resolution and resignation in my heart that I was now sentenced to die in my sins. I never quite understood what it meant to die in sin, but I knew the revelation of it now.

And so, I approached the altar and got up upon it and lay there looking up. It seemed the knife of sacrifice or whatever awful fate was before me never came though I was ready for it to strike at any moment. I was destined for Hell, and I knew I deserved it and that it was the justice of God. As time stalled, the unexpected happened. Instead of death, I was taken and shown things in heaven. There were things I was not permitted to remember and take to earth, but I do recall being shown vast amounts of treasures and jewels and sparkling gems and then my mouth uttered these words ...

"Things too wonderful for me ..."

Then all of a sudden, I hit hard as I fell and I was back on my mattress at home. I was back home! I was not in hell, praise God! I was a major wreck though. I was still convinced that I was going to be sent to hell so I grabbed my Bible and rifled through the pages to read Psalm 51 over and over and over again. The sacred words poured through me like a river. "Have mercy upon me O God, according to Your loving kindness; according to the multitude of Your tender mercies, blot out my transgressions. Wash me thoroughly from my iniquity, and cleanse me from my sin. For I acknowledge my transgressions and my sin is always before me. Against You, You only, have I sinned, and done this evil in your sight - That You may be found just when You speak, and blameless when You judge...." (Psalm 51:1-4). I could not read it enough. I was afraid still that I was doomed to hell because I knew I could not stand before God. I had been found guilty and condemned. I was sobbing over the pages and then in the midst of my agonizing, I had a vision come to me. All of a sudden, I saw my bare feet on beautiful green grass and there were stones of sapphires on the grass, shiny sparkly blue stones. I was then led immediately to a passage in Isaiah 54.

Isaiah 54:11-12 (NKJV)
"O, you afflicted one, tossed with tempest, and not comforted, Behold, I will lay your stones with colorful gems, and lay your foundations with sapphires. I will make your pinnacles of rubies, your gates of crystal, and all your walls of precious stones."

I realized that these beautiful gems and things are what I saw in heaven when I said the words, "Things too wonderful for me..." Hope then came into my heart. Oh, the mercies of God! They are so great. It took me three days to come back into this world. What I mean is: I was consumed in the revelation of God and could not adjust to this world which seemed so blithely ignorant of the riveting reality of His majesty. I had no desire to eat at all. Food was, in fact, repulsive to me. The things of the world were of little or no concern to me compared to the Word of God. I would sit in silence and awe for hours. Not too long doing this, the devil began berating me. He began tormenting my mind with thoughts of condemnation and hell. He seared my mind with hateful condemnation. I became afraid again. I called upon the Lord, asking Him why was this happening to me? I am not an ax murderer Lord, why did You have me encounter this experience? And as quickly as I asked, the verse Exodus 20:20 came to my mind, and so I read the verse and it said:

Exodus 20:20 (NKJV)
"... Do not fear, for God has come to test you, and that His fear may be before you, so that you may not sin."

And so, I saw that God had answered my prayer. My prayer that I had spoken, that I could not stop that sin issue I was having and I wanted Him to "change" me. Well, God took me up on it. He answered my prayer. He took me seriously because God takes sin seriously. I certainly was not taking sin very seriously. I had no fear of the Lord before me. I was out of balance in my doctrine. I understood the kindness and mercies of God, but I somehow had no understanding of the reality of His severity and the reality of Him Who is to be feared.

Romans 11:22 (NKJV)
*"Therefore consider the goodness and severity
of God: on those who fell, severity;
but toward you, goodness, if you continue in His goodness.
Otherwise you also will be cut off."*

I share this event because the fear of the Lord is the beginning of wisdom. There is so very little of the fear of the Lord in the world today and even our churches. I believe the next move of God will include a major dose of the fear of the Lord. In any case, in regard to this book about wisdom, the fear of the Lord is the beginning place of wisdom. If we have no fear of God, then we will miss wisdom entirely and live under a false illusion of who God really is.

Psalm 34: 11 (NKJV)
"Come, you children, listen to me; I will teach you the fear of the Lord."

Proverbs 9:10-11 (NKJV)
*"The fear of the Lord is the beginning of wisdom,
and the knowledge of the Holy One is understanding.
For by Me your days will be multiplied,
and years of life will be added to you."*

Prayer of Salvation

If you are seeking more in this life and desire to know God, then I invite you to repeat this prayer for the salvation for the saving of your soul. Praying this prayer from your heart and in sincerity will deliver you from sin through God's forgiveness. Through this prayer you will become a child of God and you will be transferred from the kingdom of darkness into the kingdom of light. When you die you will go to heaven and spend eternity with our heavenly Father.

Heavenly Father, I come to You in the name of Jesus. I believe Jesus is the Son of God and died and rose on the third day for our sins. I hereby repent of all my sins and ask that You graciously forgive me. I ask You Lord Jesus now to come into my heart and life and to be my Lord and Savior. I ask that You fill me with Your Holy Spirit. Please guide and direct me into the plan that You have for my life. I thank You for saving my soul and that I have now become Your child.

In Jesus's name I pray – Amen.

ABOUT THE AUTHOR

Karen Wells has taught Biblical truths for over twenty years and has a heart to see people gain the knowledge necessary for them to live free and stay free. She has taught the Word of God at seminars, conferences, and Bible Studies, and is a sought after speaker for those desiring a closer walk with God.

www.ingramcontent.com/pod-product-compliance
Ingram Content Group UK Ltd.
Pitfield, Milton Keynes, MK11 3LW, UK
UKHW022225230426
12048UKWH00016BA/1073